Cottages by the Sea

Cottages by the Sea

The Handmade Homes of Carmel, America's First Artist Community

Linda Leigh Paul

Principal photography by Radek Kurzaj

UNIVERSE

This book is dedicated to all those who care about the fate of place.

First published in the United States of America in 2000
By UNIVERSE PUBLISHING
A Division of Rizzoli
International Publications, Inc.
300 Park Avenue South
New York, NY 10010

01 02 / 10 9 8 7 6 5 4 3 2

Universe Editor: Richard Olsen
Copy Editor: Iris Becker
Designer: Binocular, New York
Printed in Italy

Library of Congress
Cataloging-in-Publication Data
Paul, Linda Leigh. Cottages by the sea:
the handmade homes of Carmel,
America's first artist community /
Linda Leigh Paul.
    p.   cm.
ISBN 0-7893-0495-3 (hardcover)
1. Cottages. 2. Architecture, residential.
3. Carmel, California. 4. California.
I. Title.
NA999999999999 2000
700'.0000—dc21   00-12345

Front cover photo:
Kuster/Meyer House, 1920. Photograph by Radek Kurzaj.

Back cover photo:
Walker House, 1950. Architect: Frank Lloyd Wright. Photograph by Radek Kurzaj.

The moral right of the author has been asserted.

Contents

The Cottages

Opposite, The old Hotel Carmelo became the Pine Inn and settled on Ocean Avenue, after its historic five-block journey on rolling logs, 1905.

Acknowledgments

I am indebted to John Wilson, general manager of the Pine Inn, Carmel's historical and cultural center, and to his staff, for making my visits to Carmel pleasant in every way.

I would like to thank the following people for their help and support with this project: Enid Thompson Sales, preservation consultant and founder of the Carmel Preservation Foundation; John Hicks, president emeritus of the Tor House Foundation; Constance Weismüeller, secretary of the Tor House Foundation; David Ohanesian, the angel of Tor House; Kent L. Seavey, architectural historian; Carol Spencer, chair of the Carmel Cottage Society; Clare McClure, of the Carmel Heritage Society; Arlene Hess, librarian at the Harrison Memorial Library; Amy Essick, photography historian; Jenny Watts, of the Rare Book Department at the Huntington Library; Wendy Welker, of the California Historical Society; Rita Bottoms, at the University of California, Santa Cruz; Susan Snyder of The Bancroft Library; Betty Patchin Greene and Did Greene; Marcia Kuster Rider and Colin Kuster; Margo Stipe, at Taliesen West; Kirk and Susan di Cicco, of The James House; and Doug Gooden, another knowledgable navigator.

Frances Baer and architect Mark Mills provided archival photographs of Mark Mills' Copper Spine. I owe a particular debt of gratitude to the many homeowners in Carmel for extending their graciousness and opening their homes to us and to the many architects and designers who generously contributed their time and shared their knowledge of Carmel. Also, a special salute to Carla and Jeff White and Robert Shuler for their invaluable assistance and for taking care of Richard and Radek!

I owe special thanks to Richard Olsen, editor at Universe, for his vision and for his composure; to photographer Radek Kurzaj for his wonderful work produced under incredible time constraints; and to Universe publisher Charles Miers.

Robert Paul, critic and partner, knows what it means.

Introduction

❧ Carmel, California, seems an inevitable place. Its stories are a vivid stream of people, beliefs, and events revealed in poetry, passion, and nature. For some, the tales of Carmel are sweet; for others, possibly not so. But long before poet Robinson Jeffers' polar gaze fell upon his destiny, long before he and his wildly courageous wife, Una, unknowingly reached their own "inevitable place" and gave it its emotional soul, Carmel's fate as a utopia and its hallmark of eclecticism had been decided. Carmel is one answer to the ancient quarrel between the poets and the philosophers about human life and how to live it.

❧ The houses and gardens featured in this book are inseparable from the fate of Carmel. Carmel is one of life's great enchantments. The eucalyptus-jasmine air is an invitation to take a walk down a cat-path to the beach and into a flow of long, untroubled days punctuated by soft, memorable nights. Dramatic in landscape and personal in scale, this is a place where sloping hills and the folds of canyons lean against upright cliffs that hover above a white, sandy beach. This is an intellectual and an emotional harbor—and a great place to surf. Almost a silence, a *philos*, exists that is nearly perceptible. What draws people to the village is its complex, tightly woven, often unassuming heritage. The force with which the senses are soon overwhelmed comes as a

Left, The lure and folly of the sea is captured in the design of this wrought-iron gate.

Below, Beach granite and the sea drift of an ocean wreckage make a stalwart beach bench.

Opposite, From U.S. Highway One, looking north toward Carmel

Right, Windemere Cottage is a landmark in Carmel. The maintainence of the heavily-rolled cedar-shake roof depends upon the expertise of local craftsmen.

Below, The Spencer Cottage—completed in 2000—was designed and built with respect for the "old Carmel."

Opposite, Activities at Carmel Beach, as viewed from the front yard of the Walker House

surprise. The neighborhood spreads into the trees, behind foliage and fences on the long, quiet streets near and above the Pacific Ocean. Everywhere is the feeling that this cottage and that one have a story or two to tell. A house with a past is certainly more alluring than one with no past at all, and so the cottages and gardens of Carmel invite us. After a few hours of indulging a natural curiosity, the rewards of these stories begin tumbling out. Here begins a love affair whose roots can be traced to the lore of distant and folk cultures. The allure in the air is poetry and emotion—Carmel's cultural insignia. If there is the basis for a design philosophy here, it is one that strives to house only justified beliefs and poetic impulses.

Left, Hand-carved statuette at Carmel Mission

Opposite, Peering through the Mission's front gates

Chapter One: Spanish Mission–Style Architecture

❧ Architecture never held a prominent place in early Carmel. High ideals (and just plain deals), were the driving forces of discovery. On old Spanish maps, the area that was shown northwest of New Spain was named after a fictional character in *Las Sergas de Esplandian,* a best-selling novel of the time by Ordøñez de Montalvo. The protagonist of this early-16th-century Spanish novel, Queen Calafia, was portrayed as ruler of a bronze kingdom believed to be located near an "earthly paradise." Its naming, possibly by Cortés himself, may have occurred as early as 1520. De Montalvo's tale also told of a lake of gold, reason enough to launch an expedition from Spain. Ironically, after 250 years of sailing California's shores, the Spanish lost their hold and their chance to unearth the lake of gold, as envisioned by de Montalvo, just two years and a scant ninety miles from the discovery of gold in California.

❧ The only significant early piece of architecture in Carmel was the mission founded by Father Juñipero Serra, the Franciscan priest chosen to oversee the missions of California. His first church in the Monterey–Carmel area was a stick-and-reed hut, or *enramada*. The padres were not trained in architecture and only created buildings from memories of the churches they had known in Spain. With the aid of central California's coastal Ohlone Indians, Father Serra de-

Left, Exterior corridors are the connecting passageways among mission buildings.

Below, Statue of Father Junipero Serra, founder of the mission

Opposite, From the center of the interior plaza, the magnificence of the architecture demands attention.

veloped the Mission of San Carlos Borromeo del Rio Carmelo. He taught his converts to build a mudbrick adobe mission, which by 1873 had replaced the *enramada*. Following that, four progressively more substantial structures were built on or near the original site, the last in 1793.

The efforts of the priests to replicate the calculus found in European church designs resulted in an architecture unique to the early missions of California. Structural components that had taken the Europeans generations to perfect, Serra's parish laborers learned to create in a few short years. It was,

...the intuitive genius of the Franciscans...in achieving a dignified, monumental form without relying on theory or stylistic consistency. They did so by remembering eclectically the moods and modes of Christian architecture, trusting their individual brand of monasticism and their keen instinct for effective improvisation in an unparalleled circumstance...[1]

Buildings modeled from memory can leave extraordinary architectural legacies. The designs of memory, particularly in Father Serra's California missions, closely matched the typical church style found in his boyhood village of Petra, in Mallorca: a compound enclosed on four sides, with the interior plaza surrounded on three sides by arched *corredors* that run parallel to the walls of the com-

Right, In 1879, Robert Louis Stevenson came upon these ruins. His public outcry and plea to restore the mission began a fifty-year-long restoration. The few remaining architectural elements—the original roof arch and the unusual star-shaped window—were saved and utilized.

pound and face the church, whose entrance makes up one side of the quadrangle. A typical Mediterranean design, the *corredor* was a shaded open hallway that created a cooler-air ventilation system, especially where breezes moved around corners and columns. Another borrowed feature is the use of extended eaves to prevent the deterioration of adobe walls in heavy rains. This open courtyard of the Mission style is generally attributed to Spanish and Moorish influences. However, the Franciscans had made early contact with the Aztec Indians, who revered their deities in the open air in front of their temple-pyramids. The *atrio,* then, could be seen as an adaptation of the Aztec religious courtyard and not only as analog of the atrium of early Christian basilica or the court of a Muslim mosque.

꙰ Many of the architectural features that were used by the padres can be found throughout Carmel. Again, like the mission designs of Father Juñipero Serra, many of these styles and components have been transformed through innovation, memory, and necessity. It was

Left, The craftsmen who helped restore the mission, including Harry Downie, were committed to a restoration that would showcase beautifully detailed work—all done by hand.

Serra's dream to build a stone church at San Carlos Borromeo del Rio Carmelo. Such a church, of native sandstone, was not built until 1797, nine years after his death. There, mission life lasted another forty-eight years. Services and baptisms continued to be held within a roofless sacristy before Mission Carmel, the padre's vision of an everlasting stone church, crumbled.

Fragments of the mission's ruins, those that could be carried or carted away, were incorporated into new buildings and shelters. The reuse of materials is part of architectural heritage; it is a principle of design that architecture is built upon the ruins of other cultures or eras. Tiles, ironwork, and timbers were scavenged and used in nearby buildings. Stones and ruins

were carried off and became the foundations of newer buildings and shelters, bypassing the need for an authoritative architectural integrity. Only in an indirect way can the incorporation of elements into new buildings, however many, be said to constitute a Mission "style." The features of a Mission style, per se, in the Carmel area, were so widely dispersed

Above, The Ohlone Indian patterns of diamond and chevron shapes frame a coppered window above the deep blue triangle and yellow spheres resting upon a reddish border.

Left, Strong geometric patterns—spheres, triangles, and squares—were used by the Ohlones to create this design around a Spanish prayer: *¡O Corazon de Jesus, Siempre ardes y resplandeces Encienda e ilumina el mio!*

Left, A small chapel off to the side of the church has gold painted pediments reaching toward a plainly painted ceiling of stenciled passion flowers, a Christian symbol of continuous striving to reach heaven.

that the style temporarily disappeared. For early-20th-century Carmel, there was very little that could be called a Spanish–Mission style architectural heritage. Thus vernacular architecture in Carmel had to begin again.

The collection of architectural components and details found at the Mission of San Carlos Borromeo del Rio Carmelo is a testament to struggle, faith, and learning. The catenary stone arches under roof timbers; squinches—a germinal piece of engineering technology for sustaining vaults and domes; *posas*—places for rest and prayer; the delicate asymmetry of window placement and leaded windows and grillwork; and painted ornamentation all express commitment and love of place. The passionflower (*passiflora alatocaerulea*) motif painted and stenciled on the whitewashed wooden ceiling of a small chapel at Mission of San Carlos Borromeo del Rio Carmelo is meticulously patterned. The elements of the passionflower are viewed as symbols of the passion of Christ: The crown may be seen as a halo or crown of thorns; the five stamens, the five wounds; the petals represent the apostles. Passionflower vines reach heights of thirty feet or more, a reminder to some of a continuous striving to attain heaven. At the Mission of San Carlos Borromeo del Rio Carmelo, an original inscription—*¡O Corazon de Jesus, Siempre ardes y resplandeces Encienda e ilumina el mío!* (O, Heart of Jesus, forever burning resplendent, enkindle and illumine this heart of mine!)—appears above a painted wainscoting of multicolored triangles, a form favored by the Ohlone Indians.

Chapter Two: The Arrival of the Artists

The first few years of the twentieth century saw Carmel become a budding architectural *sancturario*, with a design aesthetic still rooted in the early memories of other culture's building principles, but with an ever-increasing element of innovation emerging. No other town in America could equal the range, variety, and vitality of hideaways and houses that were sprouting in Carmel, most built by fishermen, farmers, and those who were more accustomed to building boats, barns, or water towers. Taking shape was the single largest community of vernacular architecture in the country.

Responsible for a significant part of the growth were two notable San Franciscans, Frank Devendorf and Frank Powers, who in 1900 purchased most of the available land in the Carmel area. Devendorf and Powers envisioned building a small, friendly community that they would promote as a family getaway. Carmel was still part frontier and part euphoria: a dream in the making.

Devendorf and Powers formed the Carmel Development Company in 1902 and soon mailed their first sales pamphlets. In classic advertising style, their marketing brochure was addressed "To the School Teachers of California and other Brain Workers at Indoor Employment." An invitation to escape the city or the Stanford or Berkeley campuses, for the sea-salt air of Carmel Bay couldn't have been more enticing.

Right, Xavier Martinez was a student of the San Francisco Art Association, the Paris Beaux Arts, and was a teacher at the California College of Arts and Crafts. He refused to show his paintings in New York, preferring the West. Here, Martinez is surrounded by his art, early 1900s.

Opposite, The Beardsley Room of Ira Remsen's portraiture studio, early 1900s

An excursion meant preparing for a picnic-like visit to a village with wooden planks for sidewalks and dirt streets. Perhaps, the "brain workers" sensed that

The ocean breaking on the shore was one of the foremost stimuli for the sublime, and writers and artists approached this psychogeographical site guided by aesthetic treatises on the subject by Immanuel Kant and Edmund Burke. Burke thought the human spirit derived far more benefit from the sea than from dry land. The seashore [was] a site of spiritually productive encounters.[2]

❧ Devendorf and Powers each had a knack for nurturing a leisurely atmosphere. Powers' wife, Jane Gallatin, a highly respected painter and the daughter of one of California's wealthiest industrialists, established the first art studio in Carmel. They believed that painting, writing, cavorting, and living off the land provided the deepest satisfaction a person could find. They wanted to make property affordable to poets, painters, and professors who valued the rewards of simplicity. And they encouraged all to help plant more trees!

❧ The allure of Carmel as presented by Devendorf and Powers quickly attracted a very eccentric group of thinkers who made the community home. These new residents were taken by the area's overwhelming beauty and, in some cases, by the ideals promoted in the Carmel Land Development's marketing brochures. From Devendorf and Powers' second promotion:

The settlement has been built on the theory that people of aesthetic (as broadly defined) taste would settle in a town…provided all public enterprises were addressed toward preventing man and his civilized ways from unnecessarily marring the natural beauty so lavishly displayed here.

"Carmel was the only place fit to live—it was the chosen land."

—George Sterling

Left, George Sterling loved the sting of the sea surf against his body and often doffed his clothing for the personal pleasure of time on the black granite beach boulders.

Opposite, George Sterling's cottage had a porch to read on, guest rooms and outdoor tents, a fireplace to warm the nights, and a writing hut behind the house, near his garden.

1905

George Sterling House

Jack London introduced Mary Austin to George Sterling, and it was Mary who introduced George to Carmel. George loved Carmel's environment and moved there in 1905. He built his house on a hilltop in the tract known as "eighty acres." Two boyhood friends built Sterling's house on one acre:

The two made a slow, but thorough and honest job on the house. I like its looks and know I'll be comfortable in it.

The house featured an enormous thirty-foot-long by eighteen-foot-wide living room with oiled redwood paneling. A fireplace, hearth, and chimney made from Carmel's soft-toned, striking chalk rock added to the warmth of Sterling's little kingdom in the trees. A sleeping porch and a broad, open porch were always available for guests and gatherings, discussions, and entertainment. The house was built for just such gatherings and the amusement of his many friends, among whom was the perpetual houseguest of the day, Jack London, who made himself at home at George and Carrie's when in Carmel. George described the pleasures he enjoyed at the house: *The house is on a knoll at the edge of a large pine forest, half a mile from the town of Carmel. It affords a really magnificent view of the Carmel Valley and River and of the wild and desolate mountains beyond them. I'm half a mile from the ocean (Carmel Bay), which is blue as a sapphire, and usually has great surf; here a soft wind is always in the pines. It*

sounds like distant surf, just as the surf sounds like a wind in pine trees. In Carmel, too, the air is always mild—there are many beautiful things to see here, mostly appertaining to the reefs, cliffs, and ocean. The gatherings at the Sterlings' were occasions for friends to feel the freedom of life away form the city. Picnics and hikes, camping and long parties filled the days and afternoons. Writing generally took place in the morning. London had committed to writing a thousand words a day (the mental equivalent of running ten miles a day). Kite-flying and barbecues were favorite activities. All the fun, however, brought the Carmel group criticism from one literary critic, who claimed that life there was so soft, that with all that beachcombing, the writers' brains were winding down to nothing.

1905

Mabel Gray Young's Lachmund

Mabel Gray Young came to Carmel from San Francisco. The daughter of wealthy New York socialites, she had studied voice and piano under the tutelage of Madame Schumann. In San Francisco she became a well-regarded vocalist and pianist. George Sterling introduced Mabel to the artists and writers of San Francisco's legendary Bohemian Club and encouraged her to move to Carmel. Once in Carmel, Mabel's talents blended perfectly with the growing community of intellectuals, artists, and musicians. Her small redwood cottage, built in 1905 by M.J. Murphy, became a gathering place for her close friends—photographer Arnold Genthe, George Sterling, Jack London, and Mary Austin. The interior was comfortable, with its small brick fireplace, redwood tongue-and-groove walls with built-in redwood bookcases, and exposed redwood ceiling beams.

Like many other Carmelites, Mabel had another, smaller house on her property, called a "portable." Mabel named hers the "tent-house." It was similar to the early "first-class canvas tents," used to accommodate overflow guests at The Pine Inn—Carmel's first hotel. The sides of the structure were made of canvas covered with thin cedar shakes. The gabled roof had a thin asphalt covering. The building had three windows; one was a solid-glass skylight in the roof. The flooring was made of rough-cut redwood planks.

Murphy, the builder of both structures, was a young man who had come to Carmel for a visit in 1902, and had returned with his new wife in 1904 to settle permanently. For many years, he built cottages for the Carmel Development Company. Murphy's design and construction influence became one of Carmel's architectural legacies. His favored styles and materials changed over the years, but his houses are still an important part of the flavor of Carmel.

1906

Door House

❧ Door House is exactly what it implies: a house made of doors. As the story goes, the Carmel Development Company had ordered one hundred portable tents from San Francisco. However, building materials were difficult to come by after the devastating 1906 earthquake.

❧ Mistakenly sent was a large shipment of elegant four-paneled, solid-wood Victorian doors. The enterprising John Columbus Stevenson set to work building a twenty-two-by-thirteen-foot house, of 286 square feet, made entirely of eight-foot-tall doors, set vertically and nailed top and bottom without studs. He topped it with a cedar-shingled hip roof.

❧ A wonderful example of vernacular architecture, Door House was occupied as a private residence for nearly ninety years, until 1995. Saved in the late 1990s by the Carmel Preservation Foundation, Door House was designated a "historic resource" and moved to a private site for preservation. Door House has been lovingly restored and serves its new owners proudly.

Left, Overlooking the sea at Carmel Bay, this is the house that German scholar and gentleman Arnold Genthe dreamed of having.

Opposite, Genthe's interiors reflect the sturdy features of the Arts and Crafts era.

1906

Arnold Genthe House and Studio

Not long before the city's major earthquake of 1906, accomplished photographer Arnold Genthe left San Francisco for the pine forests, cypress-dotted beach, and rolling hills of Carmel. Genthe designed and drafted the plans for his Carmel bungalow. It was the place he had always dreamed of.

I drew up the plans myself. The sloping roof, following the lines of the distant hills, was shadowed by two great pine trees, the largest in Carmel, and was supported by four large redwood trunks, with the bark left on. A wide porch looked out on the sea. The spacious studio and living room, thirty by sixty feet, with a high ceiling and two skylights, was built entirely of redwood, the rafters being not box beams, but solid redwood. My particular pride was the fireplace, which was large enough to take four-foot logs. And there was a cellar—the only one in Carmel—solidly built of cement.[3]

Genthe's cherished Carmel cellar was where his first experiments with color film and processing took place. His inspiration was the "always varying sunsets and intriguing shadows of the sand dunes" near his home. A gifted scholar, and stunningly good-looking, Genthe was a lifelong horseman, bachelor, and cat lover. His last cat, the haughty Buzzer IV, gave him eighteen years of "contented purring."

Left, Mary Hunter Austin viewed American achievement as the power to make and do, rather than the power to possess. Portrait from the early 1900s.

Opposite, Mary at work in the triangular-shaped wickiup

1906
Mary Austin's "Wick-I-Up"

❧ Legendary writer Mary Hunter Austin (1868–1934) moved to Carmel in 1905 and, with poet George Sterling, founded a writers colony. Members of this distinguished group included Jack London, Sinclair Lewis, James Hopper, and Fred Bechdolt. Tenacious as a "Teddy Roosevelt in a skirt," she was outspoken on the environment, women's rights, and Native American culture. Her actions were born of the belief that life itself, as well as creative genius, must be sustained by cultural lore. Her work from 1903, *Land of Little Rain*, was honored in January 2000 as the top nonfiction title of the twentieth century in *The San Francisco Chronicle's* Western 100 list of English-language nonfiction written about the western United States. Her lovingly written book is an observation of the wilderness and terrain between Death Valley and the High Sierras.

❧ The author did much of her subsequent writing from this platform positioned between three old pine trees. "Wick-I-Up," as Mary referred to it, was a tree house designed by one of the notable young professionals of California rustic design, San Francisco architect Louis Mullgardt, and built under the direction of Carmel builder M.J. Murphy. For Mary, who loved the American West and the wild, writing daily in her wickiup was as normal as another of her habits: walking through the woods in the dark of night.

Left, One of several entry gates on the large property

Opposite, At the top of a steep hill and past numerous rose bushes, the front door at Rose Cottage

1907

Mary Austin's House, Rose Cottage

Mary Austin lived in a log cabin, which she rented for a few years before commissioning M.J. Murphy to design and build this Craftsman-style cottage. It was here that she often entertained fellow Carmelites and friends, including George Sterling, Jack London, and Upton Sinclair. They were notorious for late-night walks to the beach, where they would sing songs (quite loudly) and enjoy a plenitude of spirits.

The house is a single-wall structure with wood-mullioned windows, a gabled roof, and exposed ceiling beams. The original design featured a bedroom and small kitchen situated just off the entryway, with a sitting room and large fireplace at the rear of the house.

Over the years the home has been extensively remodeled. Keeping the original structure mostly intact, subsequent owners added a bathroom, dining area, and, below, a fully functional second level built into the side of the hill upon which the house sits. The second floor features a bedroom, bathroom, and den, with sliding glass doors that open onto a patio overlooking a beautifully landscaped backyard featuring a small pond as its focal point. Above the patio, a deck has been extended from the original foundation.

The property was and remains heavily wooded. From the street, the view of the house is almost entirely obscured by stones, trees, and plants. The front approach is

Above, For gardening enthusiasts, Rose Cottage is a playground.

Right, Fish swim in the cool water of the backyard pond

Opposite, The front courtyard is a perfect place to sit and absorb the surrounding natural beauty.

a steep upgrade covered by ivy and rose bushes that engulf the narrow stairway leading to the brick courtyard area adjacent to the front door. The sides and rear of the house, too, are covered with plants which reinforces the pronounced sense of privacy that Rose Cottage affords its owners.

The Arrival of the Artists: Mary Austin's House, Rose Cottage **41**

Opposite, The owners have traveled the world over in search of Art Nouveau furnishings. Between the chair and sofa is a desk by Louis Marjorelle.

Above, Left of the fireplace is Mary Austin's original library. Above the fireplace hangs a pre-Raphaelite tile portrait.

Left, An original "La Libre Esthe-
tique" poster amid a variety of Art
Nouveau furnishings and an Arts and
Crafts era chair

Opposite, The beautiful surround
with Liberty-patterned upholstery
was acquired by the owners during a
trip to Scotland.

1910
Isabel Chandler Studio

There is much about the early artists who shaped the community of Carmel that will likely forever remain a mystery. Artist Isabel Chandler, known to some as Sarah Elizabeth Chandler, is one of many examples. Chandler, according to the town's oldest newspaper, local historians, and librarian, worked out of this splendid little cottage. This is considered fact. Yet it seems that no one is certain of her exact role in the the community and her artistic contributions to it.

The redwood-clad, timber-framed cottage is a magnificent example of early Carmel vernacular architecture. Designed with a floor plan of approximately five hundred square feet, the structure was large enough to accommodate a small bedroom and sitting area, in addition to Chandler's workspace. Perhaps the most engaging exterior architectural detail of the cottage is its roof. Gabled, hipped, steeply pitched, and featuring a dramatically sloped concave sur-

face area, it is unlike any other in Carmel's architectural history.

Chandler's wonderful studio was eventually demolished. Exactly when this occurred and why is another of Carmel's mysteries.

Left, Robinson Jeffers, surrounded by the stone of Hawk Tower, 1929

Opposite, The front facade of the house and its carefully kept gardens

1919, 1924
Robinson Jeffers' Tor House and Hawk Tower

❧ Completed in 1919 by M.J. Murphy and Robinson Jeffers, Tor House was the first structure built on the property. Hawk Tower, built by Jeffers in 1924, was added at the urging of Jeffers' wife, Una, whose fascination with W.B. Yeats and the towers of England led to its construction and influenced its design. The tower's ground floor features a space designated for writing and a winding stairway that leads to a marvelous lookout point at the top, offering breath-taking views of Carmel Bay, Point Lobos, and Pebble Beach. Today, both remain part of a preservation organization called Tor House Foundation, established in 1978 to oversee the entire property as a museum and to preserve its architectural integrity and historic significance. Members of the Jeffers family resided in an addition to the original cottage until 1999.

❧ With the aid of heavy ropes and horses, granite boulders were pulled from the beach below for Tor House's facade. Jeffers carefully selected each of the stones for their similarity to those he had seen on the facades of English barns. To avoid the fierce winter winds coming off the ocean, Jeffers built the cottage low to the ground. Now more than eighty years old, the cottage's exterior remains unaffected by the frequently extreme weather conditions of the Carmel coastline.

❧ Tor House's interior appointments have been painstakingly

Right, The living room was where Robinson and Una entertained guests including Charlie Chaplin, George Gershwin, and Martha Graham.

Opposite, The largest room of the cottage, the dining room/kitchen was later added by Robinson to accomodate the growing number of visitors and family members.

maintained by the Jeffers family and the foundation; most of the original furnishings remain in the cottage. The sitting room's low ceilings were designed to keep in the warmth from the fireplace. Adjacent to this space is a narrow stairway that leads to a small attic loft, which is where the Jeffers family slept. Jeffers also included a small guest room in the design for the house, a space that is the subject of his poem *The Bed by the Window*. Floor-to-ceiling, built-in bookshelves cover two of the sit-

ting room's walls, each of which house volumes collected by Robinson and Una during their lifetime. A corner window seat frames the views west to the Pacific and south toward Point Lobos.

In 1930 Jeffers added a dining room, which contains a large fireplace designed for cooking. The room's cabinetry, also designed by Jeffers, features beautifully detailed carvings. On one of the upper cabinet doors, Jeffers engraved an image of a unicorn (Una's muse). On the lower cabinet doors he painted

lines of poetry. Elegantly displayed in the cupboard is Una's collection of Jugtown pottery.

Both Tor House and Hawk Tower are reliquaries. The Jeffers collected tiny artifacts and relics from around the world, and others brought them small tokens of friendship from their own travels. These treasures are found around the house and tower, built into walls, cupboards, niches, and floors—everywhere a hand has rested.

Above, The back of the house and tower, as viewed from the bottom of the landscape that reaches the ocean

Opposite, Robinson built this cupboard for Una to contain her collection of Jugtown pottery. The cabinet shows the unicorn and hawk engravings, as well as the painted lines of poetry on the lower doors—all work done by Robinson.

Above right, The front of Hawk Tower

Right, Tiles in the courtyard at Tor House

1923
Donald Hale House

This little Arts and Crafts stone house is a splendid example of the work of another of Carmel's builders, Lee Gottfried. The house's exterior design incorporated a facade of Carmel chalkstone, gently pitched twin gables, and mullioned windows. The original twin gables, separated by an open entry court, were later replaced by a traditional front door with side windows. The courtyard was eventually enclosed and is used for afternoon tea parties and picnics.

1926

George Whitcomb House

During the 1920s and 1930s, George Whitcomb designed and built several cottages in Carmel. His lifelong love of wood and respect for hand tools is evidenced in the customized work found in these homes. This house, designed and built to accommodate him and his family, best exhibits his sensitivity to scale. Known among Carmelites as a master builder, Whitcomb lived in this cottage for many years.

Left, An average Carmel sunset

Opposite, Beyond the flowering aloe, the clear blue water and white sands of Carmel Beach

Chapter Three: Nature

❧ Carmel casts an eternal spell. It is as innocent as Opie in Mayberry or Audrey Hepburn in Rome. Perhaps life in Carmel can never be completely known. The artists and writers made certain of that by creating an arabesque in which Carmel's cultural memory is steeped in layer after layer of actual and mythical lore. Its story is told in "folk" architecture. Much like its sister city in art, Santa Fe, also left outside the flow of commerce by the railroads, Carmel's future lay in attracting a community of people who would not spend their time in Carmel "conducting business" in the conventional manner. It was agreed (even among the realtors) that the new Carmel should grow slowly. The practice of doing business was legislated into subordination to every other Carmel activity. Electric signs were outlawed, paving considered disdainful. Carmel was a village of limited means with a romantic love of nature and a dream of never changing its environment. Sinclair Lewis declared, "Don't let the Babbits ruin the town. You've got every city in the country beat!" Carmel's magical forests, perfumed *pescaderos*, and bountiful seashore offered an ideal world for relaxation. The greatest respect was for the landscape. It is the place we are forever seeking.

❧ *How its looks vary...but in essence it seems to draw on two images: the garden of innocence and the cosmos. The fruits of the earth*

Right, The original Carmel Beach bathhouse at the foot of Ocean Avenue, 1920s. Built by Abbie Jane Hunter, the beach center offered treats, towels, and happy times.

Opposite, A typical day at the beach, 1920s

provide security as does the harmony of the stars, which offer, in addition, grandeur. So we move from one to the other: from the shade under the baobab to the magic circle under heaven; from a seaside holiday to…sophisticated arts, seeking a point of equilibrium that is not of this world.[4]

❧ The natural world is the prize. Trees were planted in every era. Devendorf's practice was to be sure that one hundred trees were planted for every one that was taken down to build a cottage. Jeffers planted two thousand of his own cypresses to buffer the fierce ocean winds. Eucalyptus imported from Australia was planted everywhere. Discovering a colossal shock of sturdy, goblet-shaped *eucaplytus ficifolia* pods will delight every touring (or native) horticultural enthusiast! Pine and elm, oak and redwoods were planted to maintain a forested seclusion on each site. Trees were planted down the center of Ocean Avenue to discourage erosion. And still today, Carmel is diligent in maintaining its upper tree canopy, which consists mostly of Monterey pine, and its lower story of small trees, such as coastal live oaks and other multistemmed varieties. The urban forest is one of the most significant and remarkable characteristics of this community. The protection of healthy existing trees is among the city's highest priorities. The goal of preserving Carmel's forest landscape is to keep the feeling of cozy,

forested lanes intact. Trees of significant age, character, or location are protected. Should not the same be done with Carmel's cottages?

✍ Carmel is home to every architectural style one can conceive. The heyday of Craftsman design lasted from approximately 1905 into the early 1920s. Later, English styles such as Tudor, Cotswold, and Revival came into favor. Easily adapted to local materials, these styles, along with French Revival, Mediterranean, Cape Cod, and even Monterey and Pueblo Revival styles sprouted sporelike throughout the foggy, lush village.

✍ There are some unique designs that have yet to be identified. However, the buildings may have historical or architectural significance for many reasons. Is Carmel a poem built on the continuing lines and line breaks of older poems and stories? Is it the sandy beach of poetry, where the cultural surf is made up of the particles of lost words?

✍ Architectural relics are the guideposts in our lives. If they cannot be found, how can we possibly know our way, what to look for, or what to avoid? Carmel cabins are thought to once have housed characters in works by Jack London, Robinson Jeffers, and John Steinbeck. It is well known that London used his Carmel friends as models for fictional characters. Historical or architectural significance can be found in a six-by-ten-foot wooden rectangle with

Right, Builder Hugh Comstock's "Marchen House," constructed in the 1930s

Opposite, One of many breathtaking views from the property of the James House

one window. It might have been Sinclair Lewis' shed, or it may have once sheltered a delirious and wandering Robert Louis Stevenson. Two of Carmel's retired sea captains, Jonathon Wright and Anson Smith, once found Stevenson wandering and suffering from storm-induced hypothermia. The two captains cared for him in their cabin. Stevenson recovered and credited Wright with saving his life. Their subsequent friendship is now part of Carmel lore. Stevenson used Carmel as the inspiration for his novel *Treasure Island*, in which traces of this tale can be found.

Artifice is the homage. Each house does its part to honor nature. Many of the Carmel cottages reveal their origins from local materials. The older the house, the more natural and local the materials. Most tell of the cliffs, beach, and forests. Some speak of rocks and trees; others tell us more about ourselves.

In Carmel, houses do not have numbers. They are sought out by their names. Nor are neighborhood streets encumbered with curbs or sidewalks. There is no home delivery of daily mail. One must pick up mail at the post office. This village is, on its surface, an ideal of childhood; it is welcoming and friendly. Through personal exploration, visitors discover its ways slowly and carefully.

Left, Fishing from a row boat in Carmel Bay, November 7, 1940

Opposite, The beachfront landscape has changed much since this photograph was taken in the early 1920s. The Fishermen's Shacks are situated side by side and are the closest houses to the water.

1920s
Fishermen's Shacks

❧ On the bluff of Carmel Bay, fishermen's shacks sat looking at the sometimes-visible ocean. Many shacks along the shore were inhabited alternately by Portuguese fishermen, whalers, and, down toward the southern headland, by convicts.

❧ Henry Miller's first house in the Carmel area was a former convict's shack. The shacks were one-room, single-wall buildings that did not offer much protection from the ocean winds that gusted up and over the ridges. Their 300-square-foot interior space provided only the minimum in terms of livability.

❧ Two of the once-anonymous fishermen's shacks are among Carmel's most beloved coastal landmarks: the twin cottages, Sea Urchin and Periwinkle. For sea travelers, once these cottages were within view, they knew they had reached Carmel.

1920
Kuster/Meyer House

Edward Kuster came to Carmel after practicing law for twenty years in Los Angeles. He had given up life there to create what would become an important theater in Carmel, The Golden Bough. Kuster arrived in Carmel with his new wife just a few years after Robinson and Una Jeffers had built Tor House, and Kuster chose to build his own home on a site very close to theirs. Only a few years prior, Una Jeffers was Una Kuster, Edward's wife of ten years.

Inspired by castles he had known as a child in Germany, Kuster built his small, turreted castle with expert guidance from local builder Lee Gottfried. Like Tor House, the granite stones on the facade were pulled from the beach below and cut to size. The window- and door-framing feature narrow, vertical stones in the arch. One window is set with six convex panes of heavy, leaded German glass. The convex shape of each pane allows for a clear

view of the outdoors, but offers not a glimpse inside the house. On each side of the protected nursery, there is a small bottle-glass window, made from the bottoms of thick German wine bottles, in a spray of sea-green pastels. The original Vermont-slate roof remains and supports upper-story oriel windows. Exterior door-latches and light fixtures are constructed of wrought iron. The earliest of the forged ironwork is not identified, but later work is recog-

Right, The living room is thirty-five-by-sixteen feet with fourteen-foot high ceilings

Below, The half-turn stair that begins in the living room, winds through the library, and ends at the master bedroom

Opposite large, The door to the kitchen and bath (the painting to the left of the door is by Mrs. Meyer)

Opposite top, From the master bedroom, the library located on the half-space landing is only a few steps away

Opposite bottom, Known as "the moat," this passage leads from the master bedroom to the children's bedroom

nized as that of one of Carmel's masters of ornamental ironwork, Francis Whitaker. Whitaker created screens for the dining room and bedroom fireplaces, as well as the candelabra for the dining room. The living room fireplace has a native-tile surround in light, muted earthtone glazes. A passageway upstairs between the master bedroom and the children's room, nicknamed "the moat," features tiles along the walls with images of tall ships with three sails unfurled and a flag flying above. The simple lines of these sailing ships were created by famed tile-maker Ernest Batchelder.

༃ A treasure chest, inside and out, Kuster/Meyer House overflows with the dignity of personal attention to hand labor.

Above, This doorway, positioned off the front patio, frames spectacular views of the nearby ocean.

Above right, The turret at the back of the house contains the library and the stairway that leads to the second floor.

Right, Maintained with great care, the house's spacious kitchen has required little change in the forty years that the Meyers have owned the house.

Opposite, Untouched in the lifetime of the house, the choice of Vermont-slate for the roof was a wise one.

1922
Bark House

❧ Designed by the mother of its current owner and built by Lee Gottfried, this wonderfully unique cottage was conceived with the ocean spirit of Carmel summer days in mind. Through the bark front gate, stone and ivy carve an entrance past the trees and up the steps. The large front door opens into a spell cast in 1922.

❧ The facade of the house is made of redwood-bark boards that have been nailed to horizontal one-by-fours that are connected to heavy corner posts and beams. The structure boasts three original rock fireplaces. For the convenience of a quick dash to the beach, all rooms feature exterior doors. The original casement windows remain. Inside, the walls of untreated redwood glow quietly in the living room, which features built-in redwood benches positioned on both sides of the primary fireplace. A narrow stairway leads to an exposed sleeping loft built to accommodate two small beds. Adjacent to the living room is a sunken master bedroom with fireplace. At the other end is a guest bedroom and bath.

❧ The cottage's kitchen and dining area are the only spaces that have been remodeled over the years. New appliances have been added to make the space more livable. The owners, who retrieve and store fallen pieces from the forests of nearby Big Sur, maintain the exterior redwood-bark boards. Regular excursions down High-

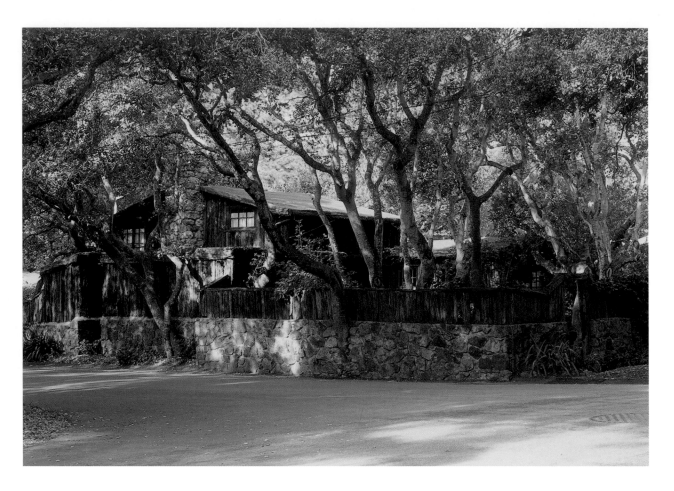

Above, Although it is surrounded by a high fence and numerous oaks and pines, Bark House is impossible to overlook when passing by.

Opposite, The living room and stairway to the loft

way One to Big Sur are a family tradition.

Bark House is situated on two lots enclosed by a rock-and-bark fence. Within this area, among the many old oaks and pines, a marvelous native and rare plant garden thrives.

Left, The desk reserved for letter writing receives natural light until the early afternoon hours and is positioned next to the doorway to the master bedroom.

Below, A window beside the front door offers views of the front garden.

Opposite, The untreated redwood of the living room walls and ceiling

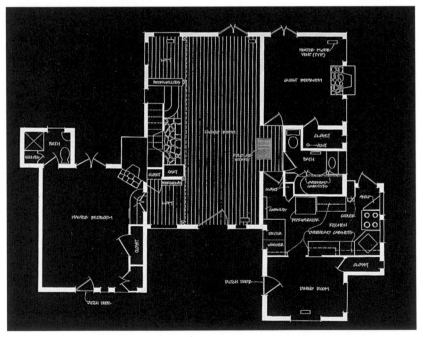

Above left, The garden-side entrance to the kitchen

Above center, Behind the window at the far right corner of the house is the study.

Above, The door to the dining room

Left, An updated floor plan of Bark House, drawn by and courtesy of Michael Cusick

Opposite, The living room (right) and the guest bedroom (left) are accessed via the house's original French doors.

1923

Seaward (The James House)

꙳ Seaward. It is the sound of a journey just unfolding. And so it is with this stone cottage, the footing of which appears to crawl down the rock face, into crevasses, gripping every available purchase. One is apt to think of it as a natural growth; any distinction between manmade and God-made is imperceptible. Seaward appears as a natural formation on the cliffscape, similar to the landscape of the Cappadocia, near Ankara, Turkey. There, cone formations resembling minarets have for thousands of years been sculpted by erosion, and excavated into residences. One might be tempted to view this highland cottage as similar to this vernacular architecture, but it is not.

꙳ When Seaward was being built, as the summer cottage of D.L. and Lillie James, it became a large part of the unfolding of Charles Sumner Greene's life of independence. The architect moved his family to Carmel to live and write among artists. The dissolution of the famed partnership with his brother Henry was nearly over when Charles was commissioned to design Seaward.

꙳ Architectural drawings could never convey Greene's demand for specific irregularities to the stonemason, so the architect's daily presence on the site was essential. Greene selected copper-tan and natural-hued stone. Roofing tiles were soft terra-cotta tones. covering and emphasizing the curves in

Right, The roots of the house are long and run deep into the landscape.

Below, It has been said that Greene supervised the placement of every stone on the house.

Left, The main living room

the roof ridge. Round terraces and outdoor stairways were paved with rock. The house became as much a natural outcropping of the cliff as if the architect had simply carved windows into the stone cliff. So completely did the materials grow together that the cottage has an almost seamless quality. In the architecture of Seaward one can find evidence of Greene's growing interests in Zen Buddhism, of the old California Mission architecture, and of architectural ruins he had seen at Tintagel, in England.

 Similar in appearance to the hand-carved, whitewashed, soft lava stone of the Cappadocia rooms, the Seaward interiors are also "carved" into soft, undulated surfaces. Greene created a mixture of light-colored shells, sand, and plaster to create curving and rounded edges within a bright and comfortable living space. Arched doorways, niche-set bookcases, and French windows allow a flow of light from room to room. The natural light in the living room draws attention to the carved-limestone capital ornaments punctuating the high cavetto moldings. Plaster butter-molds give the arches a soft "pillow-cut" appearance that reflects light from the curved surfaces to the redwood paneling and hand-carved beams.

Left, The entrance to the property

Opposite, The front of the house, captured in the morning light

1924
Hob Nob

Hob Nob is nestled under the oldest and largest remaining Japanese elm in the village of Carmel. The tree, much like the cottage that fits so cozily beneath it, lives under the protective care of a dedicated owner. Hob Nob is a Tudor-style stucco, thought to have been designed and built by one of Carmel's early craftsmen, Ernest Bixler.

Hob Nob features front and back porticoed balconies, and stonework that begins at the street and leads to an entrance terrace and an additional, arched central portico. The arch at the main entrance is a feature carried throughout the cottage design. The prostyle portico on the upper front balcony features three arches. Several simple horseshoe-arch windows (one in the loft), a large window beside the fireplace, a niche in the portico, and a tiny half-red, half-blue glass oriel high above the fireplace provide sophisticated and functional ornament. A pair of curving interior braces forms an arch that supports the dramatic sloping roofline. Stone paths race around the flowerbeds, steps, and walls.

Inside, the tracery of the curving braces gives the main living room a high central space where guests can gather for dinner, conversation, or just a quiet read by the fire. The ceiling beams are center-core redwood—ethically unavailable today. The fireplace is central to the great room. The surround, mantle, and hearth seats

are Carmel chalkstone. The chimney breast is very simply done, with white stucco that offsets the cutout staircase and loft railing at the other end of the room.

To honor their cottage, the owners of Hob Nob have a tradition of carving woodblock images of the cottage to use on announcements and invitations.

Above, The house is situated approxi-amtely six feet below street level. The stone steps in the background descend from the front gate and divide the garden space.

Opposite, The back garden and patio

1924

Hansel

֍ This tiny cottage has been categorized as a Folk Tudor. It was built in 1924 and designed to house a collection of dolls. Hugh Comstock (1893–1950), the designer and builder, met and married the talented creator of the popular "Otsy-Totsy" dolls, Mayotta Brown. Dolls overflowed their own home; therefore, Mayotta asked Hugh to build a cottage for the dolls, so her buyers would see them "in their own environment"—a fairy house in the woods.

֍ Comstock was not an architect; however, his designs invigorated the vernacular cottage style for which Carmel has received so much attention. The Comstock cottages share many architectural details, including chalkstone fireplaces with sitting stones, open-beam ceilings, and roofs covered with cedar shingles placed in irregular patterns. Comstock used economical and unconventional materials. He sometimes used heavy burlap and troweled over it a mixture of plaster and pine needles! A feeling of "fairyland" rusticity made itself known.

֍ Facing the street is the facade with its single gable and four mullioned windows, which allow the light of the setting sun to brighten the master bedroom and living room. A gravel path extends around the landscaped property to a rough stone stair with low stone stringers leading to the front entrance. The entry door is Tudor-

Left, The street-facing side of the house—a familiar place for the average tourist with camera and the occasional fence jumper in need of a close-up shot

Opposite left, Comstock's unusually shaped fireplace and the front Dutch door

Opposite middle, From the front doorway, looking to the left at the master bedroom, the center at the loft, and the right at the kitchen

Opposite right, The floors here in the master bedroom, as in the other rooms, are captured in mid-renovation.

arched and made of rough planks tied with a wrought-iron brace. Comstock hand-wrought the door hardware.

🌿 Above are two gables: the lower gable projects forward and contains the entry door; the taller, main gable is set asymmetrically behind it and appears to become a second story, with a centered, mullioned window. The rooflines are steeple-pitched and bell-cast, with hand-hewn bargeboards and gable ends. Heavy, hand-fashioned brackets support the entry gable. The roof is covered with wood shingles that are laid in an irregular pattern.

🌿 Cladding is roughly applied stucco, and wood trim at the windows and doors is hand-hewn, decoratively applied wood. A massive chimney, made of Carmel stone laid in irregular lines and peaked with an arched chimney pot, dominates the front of the tiny building. Landscaping is fir, oak, and ivy. Geraniums line the paths and fir needles cover paths and open areas.

🌿 The 300-square-foot interior—its surfaces now being refinished—features a living room with an adjustable stepladder that leads to a small loft designed to serve as a guest bedroom. The master bedroom, with its built-in bookshelves, is just large enough to contain a twin bed. The bathroom and kitchen, equally tiny, have been remodeled to include modern fixtures.

🌿 Hansel, one of the most unusual and popular houses in Carmel among visitors, is a landmark in Comstock's long career as a designer and a builder.

1925
Las Olas

The exact origins of Las Olas, like many of the early cottages of Carmel, are a mystery. The city's records are bereft of any information on an architect, designer, and builder of the home.

Carmel Historic Survey, which conducts evaluations of the area's historic homes, did determine that Edward Mestres, nephew of Monsignor Mestres of the Carmel Mission Basilica, did the facade and landscape stonework. Mestres' work on Las Olas is one of the finest examples of the charm of Carmel's indigenous chalkstone. The warm beige and praline tones found in the stone are irresistibly inviting and soft.

The cottage was designed and built in 1925. A fine example of the Cotswold style—so-called because the most sought after building stone in England is said to come from the limestone beds of the Cotswold region—the home is U-shaped. The hipped roof is finished in cedar shakes and is rolled at the edge. Because the cottage is built into the landscape, at street level it appears to have only a single-story, but a second level exists below.

The entrance at street level opens to a large sitting area with exposed redwood support beams and redwood walls, a large Carmel stone fireplace, and a picture window that stretches more than half the width of the room. Situated below the window and extending around to the corners of the room

Opposite, The kitchen has been remodeled with new cabinetry, appliances, and lighting fixtures.

Above, The picture window above
the built-in bench offers perfect
views of the ocean.

Opposite, The newly-added wine cellar features custom woodwork.

Left, The back of the house reveals an addition that is inconsistent with the house's original design.

is a built-in seat, also constructed of redwood. From here, views of Carmel Bay and its magnificent sunsets are unobscured. Adjacent to the sitting area is a dining room and kitchen, both of which have been remodeled over the years. Also on the main floor are the master bedroom, bathroom, and a small area used as an office space, which also features a floor-to-ceiling window overlooking the large backyard and the ocean. The backyard terrace is accessible from the main floor via French doors and from a wrought-iron spiral staircase that connects to the lower-level back patio area.

≈ The second floor, designated for guests, includes a small living room, two small bedrooms, and a bathroom. The latest addition to the cottage—also on the lower level—is a wine storage room, featuring handmade, custom-fitted cedar racks, and Carmel-stone floors and walls.

≈ Situated on two lots overflowing with fuchsia, geraniums, ivy, bamboo, eucalyptus, and live oak, the privacy of the home is maintained on all sides.

1926

Forge in the Forest

When speaking of their beautiful community, many residents talk of how Carmel found them rather than how they discovered Carmel. This is the nature of the place, its aura. When, in 1990, Fred Nelson and Karyl Hall bought this house, originally a blacksmith's workshop, and decided to transform it into their dream cottage, they recognized the importance of preserving the existing architecture—much of it quirky but of a high standard of craftsmanship. As time went on and the Nelson/Halls settled in, it seemed as if the house had somehow found its ideal owners.

The two-story structure and many of its appointments had aged well and had been maintained sufficiently over the years by several different owners. The ground floor contained two bedrooms and a storage area. The top floor featured a large living room with board-and-bat ceiling and exposed support beams, a large Carmel-stone fireplace, and a Dutch door that opened out to a large, second-story deck overlooking the garden. Adjacent to the living room was a small kitchen and a small study.

With the expertise of local architect Stephen Wilmoth, the Nelson/Halls went about exercising their seemingly boundless creative energy to realize their vision of their new home. On the top floor, where the original kitchen was located, a much larger kitchen space was added, completely out-

Above, The clinker-brick facade of the dining room fireplace

Left, The new kitchen

Opposite, The living room with its Dutch door, exposed beams, and broad, arched fireplace

Left, The bath in master bedroom suite

Opposite, The master bedroom

fitted with modern appliances. Adjacent to the kitchen is a new dining room and fireplace featuring a clinker-brick facade, designed by Karyl. Also on the top floor, Wilmoth designed and added a new wing to contain the master bedroom suite and large bath. Below it, he added a garage space.

The upper-level facade of Wilmoth's addition is a visual banquet of eyebrow dormers, oeil-de-boeuf and oriel windows, and bays swathed in climbing roses. English hardware gives a spot or two of ornamentation. The roof is finished with staggered-course cedar shingles. The chimneys arc crowned with ceramic pots.

The renewed cottage is made more charming by the addition in the landscape of other architectural jewels. There is the Forest Cottage, a gazebo, and Elf Cottage (complete with elves), and the famous Door House, which the Nelson/Halls helped save from demolition and is their latest project—onc that will certainly benefit from their meticulous attention to the finest of details.

Left, Surrounded by high shrubs, Our House is barely visible from the street.

Opposite, The house's manicured front garden area

1928
Our House

❧ Hidden behind high flowering shrubs, a grape-stake fence, and a small wooden gate is another of designer and builder Hugh Comstock's gems: the pink-and-green cottage called Our House. His fifth cottage in Carmel, Comstock designed and built this home just as his career as a builder was beginning to blossom. Among many Carmelites, it is considered one of the most charming of his designs. City records show that, in 1928, the house sold for $2,200.

❧ The exterior of the cottage features several signature architectural details found in Comstock's work of this period. The most notable are a steeply pitched roof with irregularly patterned shingles; hand-carved heart-shaped cutout shutters; a narrow, triple-paned arched window; an irregularly shaped Carmel-stone fireplace, a stuccoed facade over wood framing; wood casement windows; and a dormer positioned over the front entrance.

Here, as with Hansel, the front entrance does not face the street but is positioned at the side of the property.

❧ A single-wall structure, Our House's interior ceiling beams are exposed and painted white throughout, as are the walls, which are made of plaster-and-wood panels. The original floor plan remains as Comstock designed it: a broad fireplace with hearth bench, a sitting room with alcove opposite the front door, a tiny kitchen, a master

Left, The alcove is reserved for reading and the occasional tea party for two.

Opposite, The living room and its charming fireplace

bedroom, and a bathroom. The living room is built around its large stone fireplace, the massive surround of which shows off large blocks of chalkstone. Some rocks are used as niches or tiny mantles.

In the 1960s, a modestly sized addition was added to the house without interrupting the integrity of the original design. A bedroom, bathroom, and family room was added. The kitchen has been remodeled and modern appliances have been added. What was originally one of two kitchen windows is now a mid-wall passthrough to the addition. Many of the cottage's original furnishings have been reupholstered and remain in the home. When the original owner sold the cottage, she left behind her sofa and chairs, which the current owners reupholstered with Pierre Deaux fabric.

Like the house itself, the landscaping of the cottage is scrupulously maintained. Perfectly sculpted shrubbery outlines a pathway of pebbles that leads to the front door and back gate. Rose bushes on the property number in the hundreds and bloom in shades of red, lilac, and, of course, pink.

Above, When the house was remodeled, the kitchen was made more functional with the addition of modern appliances and this pass-through.

Right, When the rose bushes are in bloom, these windows are usually opened to welcome in the wonderful perfume.

Opposite, The master bedroom

Left, The charm of Sunwiseturn is in its simple details.

Opposite, The south-facing facade

1929
Sunwiseturn

Sunwiseturn is the twin to Our House. As the story goes, an efficient businesswoman named Elsbeth Rose was so enchanted with Hugh Comstock's design for Our House that she persuaded him to build a duplicate. Not an exact match, Sunwiseturn is still an exceptional cottage, not only by virtue of being a twin, but also as one of the last of the Comstock cottages to be built—completed just months before the stock market crash of 1929.

Like Our House, Comstock designed Sunwiseturn as a single-wall structure with a stucco facade and wood casement windows with hand-carved shutters. Again, Comstock designed and hand-wrought most of the hardware on the cottage. The south end of the house displays a broad chimney of irregularly placed Carmel stone; the north features an upper and lower gable, with the lower gable containing a bay window. Unlike the plan for Our House, Sunwiseturn

has a dining room, an element of the design that was added at the insistence of the original owner. There are other details here that are not part of the design for Our House: Between the fireplace and front entrance is a small chute for firewood; and French doors that open from the bedroom to a Carmel stone patio are at the north end of the house. All of the wood casement windows are original and remain in good condition. Modifications to the cottage's ex-

Right, Unlike its twin, Our House, Sunwiseturn's front door faces the street.

Below, The original business license to build Sunwiseturn, granted to Comstock by the City of Carmel-by-the-Sea. For the license, the city charged Comstock $2.50.

Opposite, The master bedroom's French doors (original) open to the patio and garden.

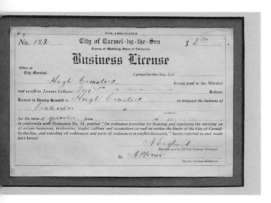

terior have been minimal, with the exception of a new redwood shingle roof, and the decorative painting applied to the stucco near the front door and below the windows that face the street.

To construct the interior walls, Comstock applied plaster over stretched and cut burlap. He used this method throughout the cottage, and it remains intact today. Interestingly, Sunwiseturn wasn't electrified until 1935. Unlike Our House, the living room alcove features a built-in daybed designed and built by the current owner.

Positioned at the top of a small, triangular knoll at the end of a footpath to the beach, the home sits in a clearing and has a signature-Carmel grape-stake fence running the perimeter of the backyard. Just beyond the south end of the cottage, a patio of Carmel stone has been laid and is surrounded by rose bushes and pines.

Left, The house's grape-stake fence and the gate that leads to a path to the ocean

Below, Floor plans and elevation drawings, courtesy of Jon R. Hagstrom

Opposite, The living room's fireplace and daybed

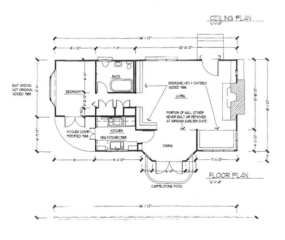

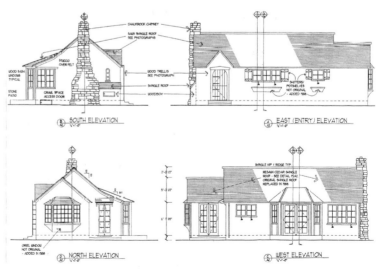

1930

Leetes Island West

❧ Leetes Island West is a cherished discovery. Percy Parkes, another of Carmel's favorite early cottage builders, left his signature on this tiny home. Parkes' cottage interiors often imitated an afternoon of relaxation in the woods (the living and dining rooms), or a morning spent in the garden sunlight (breakfast and sunrooms). Parkes' well-executed design for this cottage gives the home the appearance of being larger than its nine hundred square feet.

❧ Over the years, general upkeep of the exterior has altered the look of the cottage, but has not changed the structure of its design. Today, it features a facade of redwood shingles and metal casement windows, which have been painted white. The roof has been tar papered and covered with prefabricated shingles.

❧ The redwood-paneled living room features exposed redwood beams and ceiling-high metal casement windows, mullioned and grouped in twos and threes. The stone of the fireplace and chimney is exposed only from the floor to the mantel and is flanked by built-in shelving. The living room is comfortably furnished with a collection of New England antiques.

❧ Unlike many other houses built during the same period, this cottage contains two bedrooms: a master bedroom and a smaller, guest bedroom. A small bathroom separates the two rooms. Opposite the living room is a bright, spa-

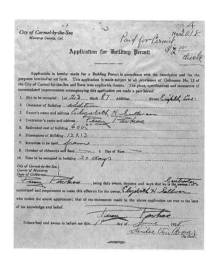

Above, Builder Percy Parkes' original Application for Building Permit, dated June of 1928

Above right, The fireplace and built-in shelving

Opposite, The living room

cious kitchen, which is appointed with rare collectibles gathered from trips across the United States. Situated just beyond the kitchen and overlooking the patio and backyard is a dining area, complete with a nineteenth-century farmhouse-style dining table. ≫ The cottage's owners, formerly of Connecticut, had been looking for a simple, wooded setting. Their new home, Leetes Island West, is swathed in elms, eucalyptus, and ivy. It reminds the couple of one of their other favorite places: a seaside retreat near Guilford, Connecticut, called Leetes Island. Each time they walk through the grape-stake gate and up the Carmel-chalkstone path to Leetes Island West, its quietness and quaintness welcome them home.

Left, Leetes Island West has an unusually spacious kitchen.

Below, When the weather is right, the dining room is extended outward via French doors that open to the backyard deck.

Opposite, The master bedroom

1931

Hasenyager House

By 1931, the year this cottage was completed, its builder, M.J. Murphy, had firmly established himself as one of the most skilled craftsmen working in Carmel. Among the many splendid homes that bear his trademarks, Hasenyager House, as it is known today, is arguably his greatest achievement as a designer and builder. Here, the wealth of talent he accumulated is evident in every aspect of the house's design. Carefully restored in 1987, Hasen-yager House is unlike any other in Carmel.

A two-story French Tudor bearing Norman influences, this elegant cottage fits into its surrounding landscape without pretension. The main roof is valleyed and the second-story dormers are hipped; the side roofs are gabled; all are steeply pitched and finished with traditionally patterned redwood shingles. At midlevel of the south side of the main roof, Murphy placed an eyebrow dormer. In the Norman tradition, he arched the doorways. The stucco facade is off-white and is complimented by forest-green steel window casements, which include a large, mullioned bay window in the living room. The chimney, one of the most interesting exterior features of the house, is tall and octagonal and marked with a decorative pargetted Renaissance medallion. The handmade ceramic chimney pot is also the work of local craftsmen.

The front entrance opens to a

small waiting area that separates the living room from the dining room. The arched doorways enclose paneled redwood doors that allow passage from each of these spaces, along with the others in the house. The fireplace is nearly five feet wide and features carefully and decoratively placed Carmel stones. Exposed hand-hewn redwood ceiling beams run the width of the long living room and dining room. From the dining room, the backyard stone patio is accessible via French doors, which are strategically positioned to allow late-afternoon sunlight into the space. The first and second floors each contain two bedrooms and a bathroom. The first-floor bedrooms are at the very back of the house. Adjacent to the dining room is the kitchen, a large space that has been thoroughly remodeled to increase its functionality. There, a small alcove with views of the backyard garden is reserved for a breakfast table for two.

Left, The remodeled kitchen

Opposite, From the dining room,
looking toward the back of the house

The landscaping of Hasenyager House is one of the most meticulously detailed and maintained in Carmel. The garden, which begins at the front of the house and extends around the perimeter of the south facade, is divided into rooms, each with its own theme. Low-growing boxwood hedges separate each room, which, cumulatively, showcase fifty-six rose bushes, lupine, forget-me-nots, batchelor's buttons, wisteria, pansies, iris, camellias, variegated wigela, daphne, plumeria, rhododendrons, anenomie, lilacs, lavender, phormium, and a tea tree, a Japanese maple tree, a sequoia redwood, and a rare Australian gum tree. Numerous garden ornaments by Andre Rognier complement the area. Protecting the house and its delicate garden is a wrought-iron fence adorned with shell ivy and a fleur-de-lis motif.

1936, 1938
Edith's House and Studio

❧ The year 1936 marked a significant turning point in Hugh Comstock's career as a designer and builder. Thus far, he had experimented with styles including Cotswold Tudor, Norman-influenced English Tudor, traditional Arts and Crafts, Shingle Style, American Colonial, and the style of his own invention and the most popular of all, Dollhouse Tudor.

❧ The Cape Cod style, in which Edith's House and Studio was built, has for years bewildered several of Carmel's most reliable sources of information on the origins of the town's residential architecture. Even among those who have studied Comstock's career in Carmel, these two structures were not recognized as a part of the Comstock oeuvre.

❧ Fortunately, in December 1999, a family member of the original owner found the house and studio's original site plan blueprints and sent them to the present owner. All of the documents, carefully kept over the years, bear Comstock's name.

❧ The house's cross-gabled roofs rest on double walls and are covered with staggered course cedar shingles. The eaves, positioned lower than most Comstock roof designs, extend slightly over a facade of Carmel stone that, at the base of the gables, abuts redwood colonial siding. Like most Cape Cod–style cottages, the house's chimney is large and centrally located. A slight departure from the

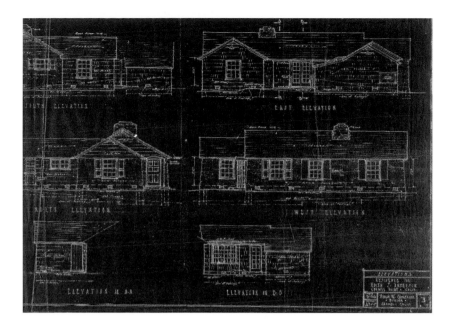

Left, The original Comstock elevation drawings, courtesy of Jane Dunaway

Opposite, Visible beyond the garden area that exists between the studio and house is the painted redwood siding and Carmel stone of the gabled side of the house; the operable, heavy shutters are painted green.

traditional Cape Cod structuring, the front door is positioned at the gable end, adjacent to a quieter side street. All of the windows are wood-sashed and, due to the house's proximity to the beach, are adorned with heavy wood-paneled shutters.

The house was conceived of primarily as a beach retreat for its owners. As such, Comstock designed a living room around the fireplace, large enough to accommodate several guests. The house also has two small bedrooms, a kitchen, and a small bathroom. From the living room, French doors with Comstock's original hand-wrought hardware open to a small Carmel-stone backyard patio. The walls and ceiling are covered with two-coat plaster.

The studio, finished two years after the house, was constructed in much the same manner. Unique features include large, rectangular, antique terra cotta on the floor and open-beam ceilings. The single-wall construction is covered on the interior with wood paneling.

The small living room contains a Carmel-stone fireplace. Adjacent to the living room is a kitchenette and a small bathroom. The studio's numerous wood-sashed windows afford the space a great deal of natural light.

The house and studio are surrounded by a rolling lawn and a painted, split-cedar fence with a four-paneled gate and lantern. The garden area that separates the house from the studio is filled with clusters of roses, passionflowers, and geraniums.

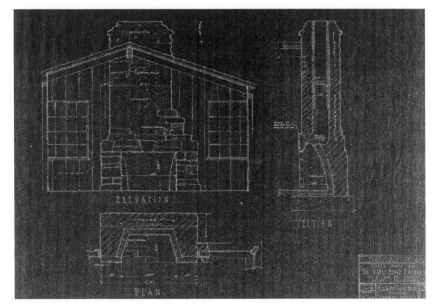

Above right, The front of the small studio

Right, Comstock's original elevation drawings of the studio, courtesy of Jane Dunaway

Opposite, The sparsely decorated main room of the studio

Left, One of the cottage's many exterior ornaments

Opposite, Once past the stone wall that extends the boundaries of the front of the property, the detailed craftsmanship that characterizes this cottage comes into view.

1940s
Rasmussen/Klawans-Smith Cottage

For nearly thirty years this cottage belonged to the Drew branch of the Hollywood Barrymore family tree, before being acquired in 1989 by master craftsman and designer David Burdge. For six years, Burdge completely remodeled the property with the intention of making it his kind of home. Using very basic tools, Burdge developed and executed some of the most creative woodworking techniques to be found in the cottages of the Carmel area.

One of the most interesting aspects of the structure's exterior is its sloping roofline with beautifully hand-hewn barge boards that extend the eaves beyond the gables by more than a foot. The red cedar–shingled roof, laid unconventionally, was designed to look old and sagging. Burdge achieved this by cutting into and building upon the original framing. The hand-hewn appearance of the barge boards was achieved by carefully dragging a skill saw side-

ways across the length of each surface. The original facade was drop siding, which Burdge later battened and skinned with resawn plywood to cover the double-wall construction. The wood-sashed bay window that looks into the dining area is also original. The windows at the back of the house slide horizontally and are also wood-sashed. The front support posts have been milled to look hand-hewn. The divided-light French doors at the kitchen area and the

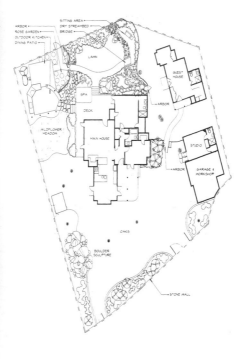

Above, Site plan drawn by and courtesy of Brian Rasmussen and Katherine Klawans-Smith, ASLA

Above right, The deck, spa, and landscaping of the back of the house

Opposite, Atop the roof is a pyramidal skylight that was salvaged from a fire at Monterey's Cannery Row.

entryway are original. The front porch is made of river rock. In the mortar are single footprints of a dog and a cat—another example of Burdge's decorative work.

The details of the cottage's interior are no less engaging. The front door leads to a magnificent oak plank floor that, like the barge boards, was given a hand-hewn look using the same skill saw technique. The floorboards extend through the living room. The walls of the entry hallway and the rest of the house are drywall that has been thoroughly textured and then painted and glazed. The dining room features a pyramidal skylight that was salvaged by original owner Greg Drew from a fire at Monterey's famous Cannery Row. When Burdge found it in the cottage's backyard, he replaced the damaged glass and installed it in the dining room to allow additional natural light. The dining room

Left, From the living room, the view of the kitchen and dining room and the Mexican saltillo tiles that cover the floor

Opposite, The skylight above the kitchen and dining room

and kitchen floor is tiled with eight-by-eight-inch Mexican saltillos. The countertops, too, are saltillo tiles, with the addition of randomly placed decorative tiles. Two handmade kitchen sinks adorn the countertops. Except those by the sink and stove, which are handmade out of copper, the kitchen cabinets are made of recycled wood and are appointed with old casement window latches. Of the many subtle yet charming details that are a part of Burdge's design, in the kitchen, inside the silverware drawer, he inscribed in ink, "I love you."

✤ From the kitchen, a broadly arched passage leads to the living room. The room's pitched fir ceiling beams have been sandblasted and stained. Two large, single-pane, plate glass windows, one at eight-by-five feet and another at seven-by-five feet, allow a plentitude of natural light into the room. The fireplace and hearth are of Carmel stone, and the sides are plaster, with one side featuring a Burdge engraving of a heart and arrow. The master bedroom area, which includes a small bathroom, is of average size for a cottage of this period. For the bathroom, Burdge hand-carved a mirror frame, a vanity, a toilet seat, and hand-wrought the room's towel bars—all of which remain in the house.

✤ Not the kind to settle in one place too long, the story goes, Burdge sold the house and is now

Left, The hand-hewn look of the floor boards was achieved by dragging a skill saw sideways across each board.

Below, The living room's Carmel stone fireplace

Opposite, The living room furnishings reveal the owners' affinity for the work of the modern era. A lounge chair by Charles and Ray Eames occupies one corner; a lounge by Le Corbusier occupies another.

Right, The master bedroom

in Belize, operating a kayak business. The new owners, one an architect the other a landscape architect, were looking for a house rooted in the aesthetic of the modern era when they found and fell in love with this house and property. In need of an extra bedroom, they expanded the original 800-square-foot floor plan of the main house (a small storage house and guest house also exist on the property) to twelve hundred feet with the addition of a guest bedroom/office. Painstakingly yet seamlessly designed and constructed using the same building techniques and materials utilized by Burdge, the addition is an example of architectural and design magic. Upon close inspection of every detail, the structure appears unaltered.

❧ The area surrounding the house is marvelously landscaped. In the front are thirteen California live oaks, a valley oak, a pear tree, Japanese maple trees, a dogwood tree, and a sculptural mound of river boulders. The sides of the cottage are heavily shaded and feature gardens filled with rhododendrons, azaleas, ferns, Boston ivy, English ivy, and hydrangeas, among other ornamentals. The landscaping beyond the cottage is the exceptional work of the landscape architect-owner. It features a native grass and wildflower meadow with California poppies,

tidy tips, thyme, yarrow, and baby blue eyes. A pathway made of Carmel stone was designed to link the patio and backdoor-accessible deck to a decomposed granite path that wraps around the lawn. A rose garden grows opposite the deck. At the very back of the property is a garden containing honeysuckle, salvia, penstemon, lavender, agapanthus, and other perennials and annuals. The small arbor, built by Burdge, is adorned with a vine called happy wanderer. Built over a dry streambed is a redwood bridge that leads to a sitting area reserved for peaceful contemplation and relaxation. And for those frequent occasions when the night air is cool and the sky is clear, a spa built into the deck is only a few steps away from the living room.

Above left, The outdoor patio at the back of the property features a fireplace, stove, and a handmade picnic table. The handcarved piece of wood that hangs above is inscribed with the words "Moon Shadow."

Above right, A wind chime hangs from an arbor in the backyard.

1940s

Gate House

Built in the tradition of the nineteenth-century vernacular architecture of the English countryside, this is one of the most mysterious cottages in Carmel. It is known to have once served as a servant's quarters, as part of a large estate. Some say the cottage was built by an old sea captain who became "locked to land" by age and fate. Other sources say Carmelite Charles Van Riper, author and real estate investor, designed and built it.

While the origins of it remain uncertain, Gate House is one of the most charming cottages in Carmel. Perhaps the most striking exterior element of the two-story design is the central hipped-gable roof with rounded eaves and gabled extensions. The north-facing facade features a second-story French window with a small balcony that is accessible from the bedroom. The east and west facades feature distinctive, arched dormers. All of the stone used on the facade was locally quarried. The living room's large, leaded-glass picture window, along with the operable windows positioned around the perimeter of the house, are all wood-casement and original.

The interior has been remodeled over the years, but has been done without altering the framing of the house. The front entryway leads to a small sitting area and, beyond it, a living room. Also on the first floor is a kitchen, which has been updated with modern

Above, Because of the extended and rounded eaves and the landscaping, from this side of the house the first floor appears to be a real challenge for anyone over four-feet tall.

Opposite, The backyard patio and garden

appliances. The second floor features a bedroom and small bathroom.

✺ Situated on four Carmel lots, Gate House's expansive front lawn offers beautiful views of the near-

by ocean. For privacy, boxwood hedges guard the front patio area. The bayed French doors at the back of the house frame views of the cottage's Carmel-stone terrace and small landscaped lawn.

Above right, The ocean views from the Gate House property are often exceptional.

Right, The cottage's roof is one of its most distinguishing architctural elements.

Opposite, Gate House's front yard is not typical of most Carmel cottages.

1945, 1986

Selner Cottage

Originally a one-story, 500-square-foot, single-walled wood cottage, the house that stands on the property today is the result of a cleverly executed remodel of the original structure and the addition of 300 square feet of living space. Built into a cluster of coastal live oaks, the renovation and addition makes use of its space in an imaginative and efficient manner. Now a cedar-shingled three-story, designed with interconnected living and working areas, the house has three distinctive spaces: "The House," "Tower I," and "Tower II." Numerous extended eaves, gabled dormers, lean-tos, and awnings characterize the exterior of the entire cottage.

The House is centrally located on the ground floor and contains a living room, dining room, bathroom, and kitchen, all of which have slightly vaulted, open-beam redwood ceilings. Skylights are in the kitchen and living room, which has a Spanish-style *fogon* fireplace with a Mexican saltillo-tiled hearth. French doors open from the living room and extend the space onto a redwood deck built around a large oak tree. The dining area, adjacent to the living room, is marked by a circa-1900 Mission-style stained-glass window and is separated from the kitchen by a pass-through wall section that houses a ceramic-tiled stovetop. The kitchen's casement windows open out to the front patio and entryway.

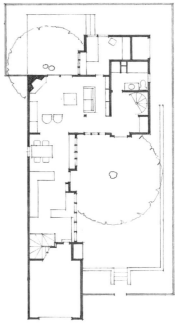

Tower I is accessed a few feet from the living room via a wrought-iron spiral stair that leads up to a midlevel office space and through to the master bedroom at the top level. French windows line the wall that separates the bedroom from another large, redwood-planked deck. The wing's bathroom is also on the top floor. Large picture windows allow natural light into Tower I.

From the kitchen, a quarter-turn stair surrounded by picture windows leads to Tower II. There, a built-in bed and bookshelf occupy one corner of the room, which receives natural light from three casement windows above. Anchoring part of the built-in is a wall that, at the uppermost half, frames a four-by-four-foot picture window. Thoughtfully designed, the positioning of the window allows framed views of The House, Tower I, and the coastal live oaks in the backyard.

Above, The Selner Cottage floor plan, drawn by and courtesy of architect Lynn Charles Taylor

Above left, The dining room and kitchen, which leads to Tower II

Opposite, The living room's Spanish-style fogon fireplace with Mexican saltillo-tiled hearth

Above right and below left, The bright and functional Selner kitchen

Below right, The master bedroom at the top level of Tower I

Opposite, The built-in bed and bookshelf of the top level of Tower II

1948
Walker House

If there is one house in Carmel that stirs a collective memory, it is the sea-burnished house on the rocks of Carmel Bay, designed by Frank Lloyd Wright. The Walker House is the only residence designed by Wright on the Monterey Peninsula and within Monterey County. In 1918, Mr. and Mrs. Willis J. Walker, of San Francisco and Pebble Beach, purchased 216 acres of land in Carmel, which included this oceanfront lot. In the 1940s it was deeded to Mrs.

Walker's sister, Clinton (Della) Walker. Della had spent many memorable summers at Carmel beach in a small stone cottage, which she tried in vain to purchase. When this stretch of beach property was given to her under the provision that she engage a noted architect to design a house there, she knew what she wanted and pursued Frank Lloyd Wright to bring her vision to fruition.

Della wanted a design that would include one bedroom, a study, a

sauna, and an entry/garage. She also wanted dramatic ocean views from every room in the house, to be as close to the water as safety permitted, and for the house to offer a great deal of privacy from the traffic of the nearby road. In 1945 she wrote to Wright, explaining her simple needs and requesting his help. Wright accepted the commission.

Situated on a mass of granite boulders and exposed to often violent storms and pounding waves,

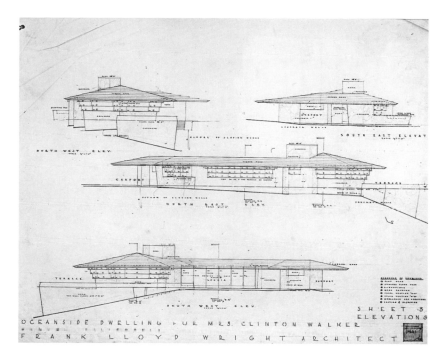

OCEANSIDE DWELLING FOR MRS. CLINTON WALKER
FRANK LLOYD WRIGHT ARCHITECT

Left, Frank Lloyd Wright's elevation drawings for the house, late 1940s. Copyright © The Frank Lloyd Wright Foundation, Scottsdale, AZ

Opposite, With Carmel Beach in the background, the house as it was in the early 1950s. Copyright © The Frank Lloyd Wright Foundation, Scottsdale, AZ

the massive triangular wedge of the foundation and terrace—similar to a ship's hull—keeps the house well anchored and protects it from strong winds. Wright chose Carmel stone for the facade, chimney, and foundation. Thin cast-iron columns support the hexagonal roof. To clad the roof, Wright originally selected porcelain enamel. Within a few years, the enamel surface broke apart when the underlying steel began to rust. The steel was replaced with copper, which lasted nearly forty-five years before it had to be replaced. Today, the roof remains covered with standing-seam copper sheets. Beneath the extended Wrightian eaves are corbelled steel-framed windows, also designed by Wright. Under the eaves, he placed sliding wood vents to allow additional ventilation.

Wright's spatial expression in this small house is achieved through asymmetry; no right angles appear in the plan. Down the driveway, past the carport, and into the house through the front door is a seemingly endless (260-degree) panorama of the Pacific Ocean, the horizon, and Carmel Beach. The floors are red-tinted poured concrete. The living room, like the rest of the house, is compact and features an informal, built-in dining area that wraps around a massive central fireplace. This part of the house looks very much like a captain's bridge. Wright harnessed the concepts of kitchen,

Right, The carport and front entry

Below, A letter from Wright to Della Walker, December 8, 1952. Copyright © The Frank Lloyd Wright Foundation, Scottsdale, AZ

Opposite, The driveway gate, the Carmel-stone wall around the property that borders the street, and the surrounding tall trees and thick shrubs no longer provide a real sense of privacy. After all, this is a Frank Lloyd Wright house.

Dear Mrs. Della Walker: Have just made the long anticipated visit to the little Cabin on the Rocks. Enjoyed it all with few reservations. Chief among them, your absence. Wish I might have had you there and been able to help you in the process of absorbing your cabin and being absorbed in it. Some encouragement both ways was manifest.

I hope this tiny aristocrat among the Carmel bourgeois so exciting in itself is not only a domestic experience giving you the joy you, its progenitor, deserves, but a spiritual uplift.

To build anything in these ambiguous times is bound to be either a foolish or heroic event. But your heroism is on record now at Carmel. The place should be grateful to you for this all too rare kind of patriotism, a fine thing to do with money. Vulture has its patriots. Your cabin will for several hundred years proclaim you as a competent one and I hope the sacrifice to get an original pearl is not to be too great.

I like your roof. It is even better than copper and costs no more. I like the fireplace. But remember it was designed to burn pole wood (easiest of all to get). But, I see you have piled up thick cord wood with slender sticks six or seven feet long and let the poles blaze all the way to the top. The blazing poles will then take care of the high draft and very little smoke will come to annoy you. Of course treated as an ordinary fireplace it is bound to smoke.

I liked the pile of Pacific green glass balls in the sweep of the windows and suggest you get more, big and little, pile them up in the stone bowl at the entrance with a light down in among them . . a subdued glow of light at at the gate.

The change to double bed in your own room needs some adjustment. Will design a corner feature to take the two beds? They are unnecessarily high : One bed can be used (if lowered) for a seat at the dining table or the seat moved one side and the shelf widened to make a proper table top.

Evidently the road fence fell short of your ultimate lot line. I intended it to go all the way along the road to your lot line. Perhaps planting as originally expected can ultimately accomplish the privacy you : to gain at this extension of the l t.

I missed seeing you as apart from Architecture I always do enjoy a talk wi you.

With great affection nand good hope

Frank Lloyd Wright

December 8, 1952

pantry, and the servant's space into a single economical workspace. Adjacent to the living room and behind a pleated, folding door (a feature Wright often used), the workplace looks out over a light-filled gallery. Just off the gallery are two very compact guest rooms and, at the very back, the master bedroom.

For the past fifty years the house has required little restoration. Other than replacing the copper roof and a few windows, Wright's design has successfully endured the punishing winds from Carmel Bay and relentless spray from the surf slamming against the granite below. On his original sketches for the house, Wright referred to the structure as "a cabin on the rocks." In a letter to Mrs. Walker, he stated his hope that his creation would last for at least "several hundred years." The fortunate few who have toured the house would likely concur with him.

Above right, An early sketch of the
design for the Walker House, late
1940s. Copyright © The Frank Lloyd
Wright Foundation, Scottsdale, AZ

Right, Wright's site plan for the
house, late 1940s. Copyright © The
Frank Lloyd Wright Foundation,
Scottsdale, AZ

Opposite, Wright designed the
kitchen to be compact but functional,
early 1950s. Ezra Stoller © Esto. All
rights reserved.

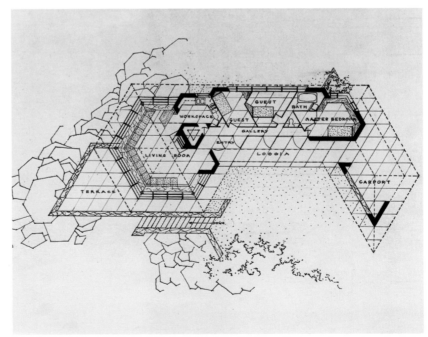

Right, The fireplace, designed to burn pole wood stacked vertically against the back of it. Ezra Stoller © Esto. All rights reserved.

Opposite, The living room with Wright's built-in seating and corbelled steel-framed windows. Ezra Stoller © Esto. All rights reserved.

Above and Opposite, The house during the setting of the sun

Left, The original designer's insignia on an exterior wall near the front door

Opposite, A dream house realized

1980

Stonewood

❧ During the late 1970s and into the early eighties, a great admirer of Frank Lloyd Wright named Erik Nielsen, a skilled designer and carpenter, designed and built this living space on a stretch of oceanside property on the outskirts of Carmel. Nielsen shared Wright's belief that a house should at the very least grace its site; if designed properly it should become one with it. He also firmly believed in Wright's Usonian principles of house construction, which influenced his work here. Memories from his visits to Taliesin West also guided Nielsen as he designed this magnificent home.

❧ Those who are familiar with Wright's work will immediately notice many Usonian features in the 1,800-square-foot Stonewood. The most obvious of the Wrightian appointments include the long, low-pitched, hipped roof with generous eaves; the carport; the absence of paint; the wood-casement door-height picture windows surrounding the large living room; the built-in sofa; the alcove-positioned dining area; and the location of the kitchen—adjacent to the living room.

❧ To execute his design Nielsen worked side by side with local builder Dale Sutton. With nearly seventy tons of Bouquet Canyon Stone and the method of masonry construction that Wright used at Taliesin West and often referred to as "desert concrete style," they built the support columns, walls,

Right, From this angle, the house appears deceptively small.

Below, The dramatic line of the eaves from the carport to the chimney

Opposite, A Steinway baby grand piano and a love seat and chair, custom-designed by Robert A.M. Stern, occupy space in front of the living room fireplace.

and the massive walk-in fireplace. Where stone is not used, Nielsen applied old-growth redwood boards that he had milled specially for the house. Vermont green slate shingles the roof.

The main entrance—strategically positioned at a long hallway that separates the bedroom from the kitchen and living room—is accessed via a solid mahogany door that pivots on a hidden, custom-designed hinge. Extending the length of the hallway are operable windows that provide views of the cliffside landscape and ocean. Below the windows, bookshelves are built into the exposed support columns.

Stonewood's interiors are rich in warmth and color. Pigment-stained concrete floors stretch throughout the living space and extend out to the patios. For the Wright-inspired board and sunken batt wood pattern of the ceilings and walls, Nielsen applied the same redwood used on the house's

Above left, The red mahogany plywood table and built-in sofa, designed by Erik Nielsen

Left, A small section of the beautiful gardens at Stonewood

Opposite, The hallway that connects the master bedroom to the bathroom, kitchen, and living room

Right, The kitchen

Below right, The Nielsen sofa and stool, with the ocean in the background

Below, The living room of the small guest house also contains built-in furniture, such as this daybed and coffee table.

Left, The master bedroom

exterior. The spacious kitchen features Nielsen's red mahogany plywood cabinetry and shelving work. All of the cabinet handles, also designed by Nielsen, are made of brass. All doors are hung with brass piano hinges. The living room's built-in sofa, another Nielsen design, is constructed of red mahogany plywood.

In 1984, at the intersection of the carport and the living space, a small guest house was added. De-signed with great respect for the existing structure and site, the space contains a small living room, a bedroom, bath, and a small space for laundry appliances.

In 1998, Nielsen sold the house to another admirer of Wright and a lover of architecture and the sea. With the change in ownership came alterations to the house, most notably the addition of a small fireplace in the master bedroom. Under the new ownership, the house has become a corporate retreat for individuals and organizations dedicated to the global improvement of human conditions. Named Stonewood Foundation for Humanitarian Initiatives, a website — www.stonewood.org — has been established for those interested in learning about this inspirational place and its special purpose.

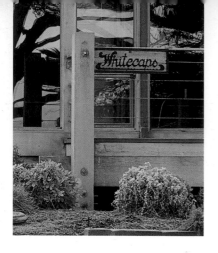

Opposite, The front facade. Just beyond the large picture window at far right the owners keep a large telescope for viewing sunsets and starry nights.

1980

Whitecaps

❧ Carmel architect David Allen Smith created a design for this modern cottage that, unlike many other Carmel cottages of this period, blends harmoniously into the landscape. Situated on a well-traveled street that borders the beach, the house's front facade is always within plain view, which, according to the architect, makes an even greater case for using building materials that do not overpower the natural surroundings.

❧ For the street- and ocean-facing facade, Smith combined bleached western red cedar and floor-to-ceiling picture windows. The fixed-glass windows mirror the trees, sky, and ocean; the bleached cedar blends marvelously with the trunks of the surrounding cypress trees and the street. Whitecaps is so close to the ocean that large waves and gusting sea breezes often cast a salty spray over the cottage, giving the cedar a sea-wracked look that belies the age of the house.

❧ A two-story house distinguished by open interconnecting spaces, the 1,800-square-foot structure is framed with heavy Douglas fir beams (mostly exposed) and has plaster-coated walls with cedar trimming. The living space is composed of two bedrooms, two-and-a-half baths, a large living room, a kitchen, and a dining room. The kitchen and dining room, both spacious, are positioned off the front entryway, which leads into the dramatic living room. Here,

Left, The dining room

Below, The backyard patio and garden

Opposite, The living room with its exposed, interconnecting support beams

the architect placed two sets of sliding glass doors that situate the space between picture-perfect views of Carmel Bay and a backyard flower garden. In between is a large, terra-cotta fireplace and hearth that separates the living room from the first-floor bedroom/office.

❧ Outside, lichen-colored groundcover and mosses border the stones and steps that climb the front entry path to the larger, shade-loving shrubs. Surrounding the back patio are native grasses. Primula *(primulaus varis)* grows under the semi-shade of lemon trees; flowering vines tower above a trellis. Between the aggregate-concrete stepping stones near the patio, Corsican mint ground cover is occasionally crushed, releasing a whiff of herbal menthe into the fresh air.

❧ Whitecaps is unique in another way: The cottage has a companion house across the courtyard, Nightcaps.

1995

Nightcaps

Conceived of as a getaway for the children and grandchildren of the owners of Whitecaps, Nightcaps, designed by David Allen Smith, is an *L*-shaped, gabled-roof, four-room house with a spacious living room, kitchen, bathroom, and bedroom. Six-foot-tall, steel-framed picture windows extend the perimeter of the house, affording the 1,200-square-foot space a much larger feel and, most importantly, plenty of natural light and perfect views of the ocean in every room.

From the landscaped front terrace, French doors open to a hallway that separates the bedroom and bathroom from the kitchen and living room. Here, as at Whitecaps, terra cotta covers the floors and bright white plaster coats the walls. The ceiling, vaulted throughout for an added sense of spaciousness, is clad with Douglas fir sheathing boards and contains the cottage's recessed light fixtures. An alcove that extends toward the ocean marks the living room, which contains a large fireplace. Cedar cabinets and decoratively tiled countertops add a sense of warmth to the kitchen.

Nightcaps' front courtyard is beautifully landscaped and shaped by twelve-by-twelve-inch, glazed terra-cotta tiles and redwood beams. A short path of pebbles links the younger Nightcaps to the elder Whitecaps. When the family is in full force and the weather is fine, the living spaces of the two cottages become one at the patio area.

Left, The kitchen and the hallway that leads to the bathroom and master bedroom

Below, The living room

Opposite, The front courtyard

1990
Stone House

❧ Of the many charming cottages in the Carmel area that have been built or rebuilt in the past decade, few possess the level of artistry found in the architectural details of Stone House. Designed in the cottage style common to the Normandy region of France, the house is the realized vision of its owners Carla and Jeff White. Carla, along with architect Bryan Addicott and contractor Rick Griffey, worked tirelessly to create a living space that is grand but not overstated.

❧ The cottage comprises over one hundred imported reclaimed materials and architectural artifacts. The sea-weathered appearance of the facade stones is the result of having each stone tumbled by hand. The roof, gabled with open eaves and marked by a link dormer supported by exposed king-truss beams, is covered with terra cotta tiles laid in an offset pattern. Custom made for the house, the roof tiles were manufactured in fifty-four subtly different hues. The oak chosen for the hand-hewn truss beams was reclaimed from an old barn in New England. All of the steel-framed windows—many of them operable—were reclaimed from old buildings in France. The doweled oak batten boards of the front door were also reclaimed. The hinges and latches on the front door are of forged iron. Typical of a Normandy-style cottage, all of the door and window openings are arched according to the common French radius.

The front entryway leads to a centrally positioned waiting hall situated between the living room, master bedroom and bath, kitchen, dining room, powder room, and a stair to the lower level. Above the ochre colored hexagon pavers (reclaimed from the French region of Percheron) that adorn the floor of the hall is a magnificent transom, acquired in Bordeaux. The living room has twenty-foot-high ceilings and is sunken a foot. Appointments here include reclaimed antique wormy chestnut-wood floors, hand-hewn hemlock and oak exposed truss beams, a wide fireplace facaded with the same stone used on the exterior of the house, and, at the back of the room, a wall of antique steel-framed windows and glass doors. The master bedroom also contains hemlock truss beams, which glow

Right, The twenty-foot-high ceilings of the the living room

Below, The living room fireplace

Opposite, The dining room's Welsh-wood table perfectly compliments the antique wormy chestnut-wood floors.

Above, Among the many fine antiques and collectibles displayed in the kitchen, Carla's extensive collection of Portuguese Palissy Ware is a highlight.

Above right, All of the kitchen countertops are surfaced with Delage Chateau flooring.

Opposite, The steel-framed doors that connect the living room to the back patio

in the light that, during the setting sun, peers through the room's antique steel-framed operable windows. The large master bath area includes a soaking tub and a turret shower built of cluny limestone. A small Gothic window admits natural light into the shower area.

～ The kitchen, like the entry hall, is floored with ochre colored hexagon pavers. The custom cabinetry is antique wormy chestnut. The

countertops are honed French limestone. The exposed hand-hewn truss beams are reclaimed hemlock. An antique steel-framed, glass Dutch door is at the back of the kitchen and provides access to the back patio. A wealth of natural light enters the area through reclaimed German water glass, which was meticulously set in the kitchen's steel-framed windows.

～ Because the cottage is situated

Right, Carla's collection of Majolica pottery surrounds the top of the soaking tub in the master bedroom suite.

Below, The straight-run stair from the main level to the second level is characterized by the arches in the ceiling and by its suspended curtail.

Left, One of two lower level guest bedrooms

on a lot with a steep gradient that slopes downward from the street, the lower level is built into the landscape. Here, there are two small guest bedrooms, a bathroom, and a small entertainment room. Both of the guest bedrooms have steel-framed glass doors that open onto the lower-level back patio and garden area.

The landscaping at the front of the house, also designed by White, is tastefully appointed with Japanese maples, Australian tree ferns, and an old wheelbarrow full of hydrangias and fuchsias. The stone pathway that leads to the front door is lined with rosemary and lavender.

Despite the meticulous attention given to every detail of this cottage (and the overwhelmingly marvelous results), the Whites still consider it a work-in-progress. Having endured the hectic pace of life in New York City and Los Angeles, they recognize and appreciate the simplicity and pur-ity of life in Carmel. The magnificent cottage they added to the Carmel landscape stands as a symbol of this appreciation and as an acknowledgement of the importance of preserving the architectural integrity of Carmel.

Left, The site formerly occupied by the Donati House, a 1924 Arts and Crafts cottage.

Opposite, The gate and path that once led to the Donati House. Japanese copper lanterns sit atop Carmel-stone posts. Each post is inset with a celedon glazed Chinese tile on point.

Chapter Four: Carmel's Fate of Place

~ *Nothing has an enduring place, except insofar as its place is determined in our minds.*

— René Descartes

~ *It is not on any map; true places never are.*

— Herman Melville

~ *How will we know it's us without our past?*

— John Steinbeck

~ *It has been said that all things must change. It has been said that one's fate cannot be changed.*

— Conventional Wisdom

~ Carmel is a small place. Its beauty and mystery are woven of landscape and lore, architecture and the sea. Carmel's first viable economy brought influences from fishing communities all over the world. Vernacular architecture from countries as diverse as Portugal, the Netherlands, Japan, and Ireland has left its mark on Carmel. Thus, Carmel was born from the sea. What architectural legacy would Carmel have if its beloved landmarks had not enjoyed this international influence? What cultural legacy would Carmel have if its first settlers and citizens had not been world travelers? And more directly, what aesthetic identity could Carmel have developed if the cottages the settlers built in their own homelands had not been valued?

~ Those aspects in our environment that create reverence form our sensibilities. Robinson Jeffers saw clearly that buildings may be built and will subsequently or

eventually decay, but the nature of a place never changes when one knows why one is there, or knows that one belongs in a certain place. Carmel is home to poets, painters, thinkers, musicians, dancers, and writers. It is home to those who share a creative and simple spirit. A love of heritage and adventure, and a reverence for the environment have always been the raisons d'être among Carmelites.

Above, The owner of the lot claimed, "We will win, we will tear the house down, and we will build what we want."

Left, The front facade of Sea Urchin, before the demolition efforts

Opposite, The roofs of Sea Urchin and Periwinkle were the first parts of the cottages to go as part of the demolition, April, 2000.

1930s

Sea Urchin and Periwinkle

In many ways, the story of Sea Urchin and Periwinkle (formerly known as Fishermen's Shacks) is the story of Carmel. These two small, Mediterranean-style cottages, a snug 415 square feet each, began as simple board-and-batten shanties. Early photographs show them as quite primitive, isolated and, as they are built upon the edge of a low cliff, exposed to the weather. They had very few windows. Old wood-burning stoves allowed for cooking and some warmth against the cold. The buildings existed without plumbing or electricity for many years; the first building permit for work to make improvements on them is dated 1930. This work may have been done for one early owner, Sarah Worcester, who bought one cottage for her own use and the other for her sister.

Steadily, small improvements helped the shacks evolve into charming twin cottages. Worcester bought adobe bricks and had workers stack it against the single-wall construction of each cottage and around each cottage's chimneys to add strength and a balanced appearance. The exteriors were finished with stucco.

By the mid-1960s, another owner added a basement, driveway, and garage. Each cottage was enhanced with a small, slightly inset entrance and tile porch under the an extended eave. Other exterior work included the addition of terra-cotta tiles to the roofs, refur-

bishing the articulated, arched French windows and entrances, tiling floors, and adding sheet rock to painting interior walls.

For the past fifty years Sea Urchin and Periwinkle have brightened the landscape and enriched the character of Carmel's architectural and beachfront identity. Each cottage's name proudly graced the space above its front door. Adored by most Carmel residents and known to visitors from around the world, these twin cottages are California coastal landmarks. Their crisply maintained white forms and bright russet rooflines capture the hearts of passersby and announce to visitors that they have arrived at Carmel Beach.

Today, despite the valiant efforts of Carmel's preservation organizations, the twin cottages risk being demolished to make way for a new house. With property values at the highest point in Carmel's history, the preservation of such simple but important architectural landmarks as Sea Urchin and Periwinkle, sadly, is a slowly growing effort.

Left, Surrounded by a garden of wild-flowers, this area was reserved for outdoor entertaining. Photo by Morley Baer, from the private collection of Mark Mills

Opposite, The living room windows offer an unequaled framing of the shoreline and ocean vignettes. Photo by Morley Baer, from the private collection of Mark Mills

1965

The Farrar House (The Copper Spine)

If he could have had it floating on the water, he would have. —Mark Mills, on the original owners' infatuation with having their house as close to the water as possible.

Mark Mills is one of several innovative young architects who studied under Frank Lloyd Wright at Taliesin West during the mid- to late-1940s. Throughout his four-year stay, Mills often sat in on Wright's routine Sunday morning talks. Wright often spoke of seashells, of the way the "homes"

of creatures are formed from the "pure joy" of their interaction with their environment, the ocean currents. These discussions were not lost on Mills.

Shortly after leaving Taliesin West and relocating to Carmel, Mills was tapped by Wright to assist with the construction of the Walker House. His work there led to other design commissions in Carmel, in the Carmel Highlands, and in Big Sur. Perhaps the most architecturally significant of these,

however, is the house known as the Copper Spine, built in the Carmel Highlands at the edge of the Pacific Ocean.

On an eroded granite knoll with a swale covered by succulents and lupine, Mills was asked to design a home that would provide spectacular views of the ocean from every room; a home that could endure the harshest of weather conditions—fierce wind, monstrous surf, and the occasional earthquake. Mills conceived of an unprece-

Left, The house, situated on the knoll beyond the granite outcroppings in the foreground, was as rugged as its site. Photo by Morley Baer, from the private collection of Mark Mills

Opposite, On a few occasions, the house's proximity to the water allowed the raging surf to wash over it. There were never any leaks. Photo by Morley Baer, from the private collection of Mark Mills

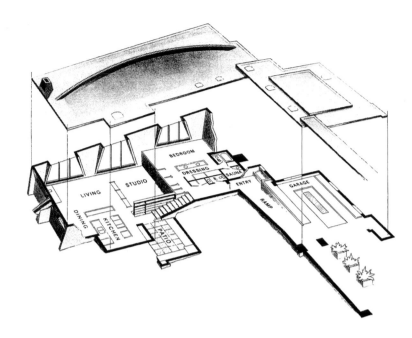

dented concept for the structure, one that would prove to be perfectly suited to its rugged site.

◦ Protecting the interiors are nine-and-a-half-inch-thick walls made of steel-reinforced concrete. To maximize interior space and lessen the impact of wind on the house, Mills sloped the concrete walls at an angle of eleven degrees. To further protect the walls, he placed them on specially made cushions and hardpacked dirt. To add texture to the exterior of the concrete, he had it ribbed and bush-hammered. The trapezoidal windows and doors were all steel-framed.

◦ The roof that Mills designed was considered indestructible. Overhanging and arched with a 26-inch-thick beam of laminated Douglas fir that was copper-sheathed to protect it from the salt water, the roof's surface was gravel-coated. The beam was connected to the walls by a ceiling composed of over a thousand two-by-three-

Above left, Drawing showing the floor plan with the roof elevated

Opposite, Constant motion surrounded the studio, which is stepped-up and separated from the living room by low built-in shelves. Photo by Morley Baer, from the private collection of Mark Mills

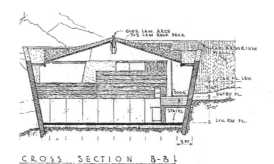

CROSS SECTION B-B'

LONGITUDINAL SECTION A-A SCALE: 1/8"=1'0"

inch boards. A pin hinge at one end and a roller bearing at the other anchored the arch, which spanned from the eastern to the western end of the house. Mills designed the roof in this manner because he believed that to endure strong gusts coming off of the ocean, the roof would need the flexibility to adjust to the heaviest of gales.

⚬ The open interior plan, free of floor-to-ceiling partitions, consisted of a primary living space containing the living room and fireplace, dining room, kitchen, and studio. The master bedroom area, elevated approximately two feet from the primary space, featured a dressing area, bathroom, and sauna. In the living room, Mills designed built-in window seats and sofas. The small kitchen area was appointed with his custom cabinetry. Poured concrete was chosen for the flooring. The ex-

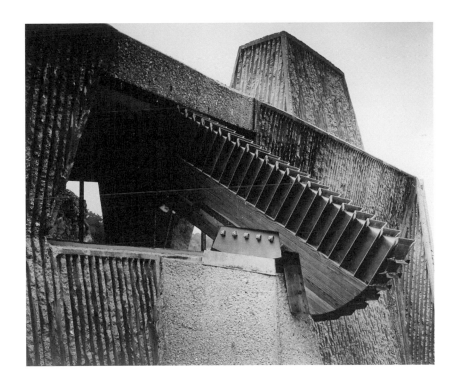

posed concrete walls were sand-blasted to bring out the features of the imbedded stones.

Compact but functional, Mills' split-level design efficiently utilized every inch of available space. Each room offered western views of sea rock formations, tidal pools and distant coastal cliffs. Proof of the integrity of Mills' design, the house withstood a 7.0 earthquake; neither the house nor its contents were affected.

Following the deaths of its original owners, the house was sold outside the family. According to Mills, it was purchased by an "over-the-hill, completely nuts but still going rock star." Only a few years later, the Copper Spine was sold again. In 1996, before the community could organize a protest to save the landmark, the house was demolished with dynamite. "The man came from Texas, and what he did is frightful," says Mills.

The ultimate fate of the Copper Spine was the result of the actions of the same mindless advance that Robinson Jeffers fought against in Carmel throughout the latter part of his lifetime. *Jeffers spent his last years fashioning an invective against the civilization that was building a road on his cliffsides and ruining the primitive life of hawks, wild boars, and poets.*[6]

Left, Detail of front door showing Greene's hand-carved images of climbing tomato vines

Opposite, Subtle as a pine cone in a tree the House and Studio occupies its site with great dignity.

1921, 1923

Charles S. Greene House and Studio

❧ In 1916, when Charles Greene, of the now-legendary Arts and Crafts architectural firm Greene and Greene, pulled into the quiet village of Carmel while driving with his family from San Francisco to Pasadena, he found a setting without peer—one that fostered artistic development and openly permitted and even embraced freethinking individuals. Two years later Charles and his family left Pasadena and settled permanently in Carmel.

❧ The studio, the second structure Charles built here for himself and his family, is situated directly in front of the site where he built his first—a simple, redwood-framed bungalow that was never quite completed. Unlike the circumstances affecting construction of this house, Charles had a number of building materials resources to turn to for help with the studio. Already at his disposal was an abundance of used brick, which Charles had acquired after a hotel

in nearby Pacific Grove had been demolished. In addition, because construction on the James House was complete and there were roofing tiles leftover from the project, he was able to use them here. For wood he turned to his friends at the White Lumber Company, the San Francisco–based firm that Charles used for all of his Northern California projects. In return for all of the business he had brought them, they provided him oak and teakwood at no cost.

Above, Greene put scrap materials to good use by creating a granite, slate, and tile mosaic border around the entry foyer.

Above right, The arches of the courtyard fence are reminiscent of Spanish *corredors* and are found throughout the House and Studio.

Right, Greene's personal touch is evident at every turn. Here, bits of tile placed where the arches meet the pediments offer a relief from the brickwork.

Left, The courtyard and Did's 1965 addition to the studio, designed as a tribute to the work of his father

Below, Did designed the addition with extended timber outriggers and low eaves—both classic Greene and Greene building traits.

❧ With renewed ingenuity for the creative reuse of materials, Charles proceeded to build. The exterior-facade bricks were set in a modified Flemish cross bond with flare headers. The arched, intricately carved, teak front door is held by a frame of brickwork set in a garden-wall bond design. For light, Charles designed at the front of the studio arched bottle-glass windows; a rectangular bottle-glass window; an oriel window; two oeil-de-boeuf bottle-glass windows; and an inset window

niche. Perhaps the most brilliant of all Charles' window designs here is the twelve-panel skylight in the open-gabled roof. To support the open-gabled roof, Charles used heavy beams that he hand-carved before positioning them on large blocks of limestone, visible at the top corners of the studio ceiling.

❧ Beyond the carved teakwood front door is an entryway with an intricately laid floor of marble framed by remnants of granite, limestone, and mosaic tile—all

Left, The hearth of the Greene Studio. The portrait above the fireplace, which dates to the 1820s, is of the first architect in the Greene family.

Below, Detail of Greene's stamping in the plaster of the walls

Opposite, The original studio space— elegantly furnished and beautifully maintained by Betty and Did Greene.

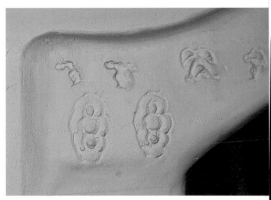

bits and pieces collected from other projects. The flooring throughout the rest of the house is oak. All of the wall surfaces are plaster, which in several places exhibit patterns that Charles pressed in using handmade woodblock stamps in the shapes of flowers, leaves, and shells. As in the James house, the walls are colored with a mixture of sand taken from the ground and mixed into the plaster. The doorways linking the interior spaces are arched; the teakwood doors are finished with Charles' subtle yet beautiful hand carvings.

The original design for the studio consisted of the entryway, a small bath, the large studio space, and a study, which often served as a bedroom. This went unchanged throughout the remainder of Charles' and wife Alice's lifetimes. Here, Charles successfully established a haven for local artists. Piano recitals were common, as were meetings to study Buddhism and the works of

Left, On an overcast day, looking at Point Lobos from the desk in the master bedroom of Cypress Lodge

Opposite, A real Carmel sunset

Conclusion

When Carmel's village lots began to sell around 1902, it was expected that the town would grow into a community of self-styled individualists. With the increasing influx of artists, reformers, and environmentalists, and its atmosphere of eclecticism, the community was a kaleidoscope of interests and excitement. Artists spent the early part of the day at work. The locals and a touring population gave afternoons over to sightseeing and playing on the beach.

Evenings were occasions for gatherings: good food, wine, and conversations, and song that often lasted long into the night. People came to Carmel for what was to be found there, not to change it.

For the past one hundred years, the architecture of Carmel has drawn a portrait with a sense of place. As each cabin was built on a knoll or reedy dune, and cottages were built in forested plots or on grassy moors, newcomers brought with them a soul-lingering love and remembrance of their own heartlands. They brought their own type of "everlastingness." Their emotional treasures were reserved for special occasions, especially those where neighbors celebrate and perform useful activities. They would gather around the hearth and repeat stories that Yeats told about Homer, or help till a neighbor's garden plot, or rehearse for a theater production.

Carmel is a community based on ritual. Beginning with the bohe-

one more of Carmel's long-held rituals. Its context is the absence of sidewalks, home mail delivery, parking meters, streetlights and traffic signals—Carmel traditions. These are the features that make Carmel a distinctive community in our country. Why would anyone want to change this historic city into the sort of place that can be found by pulling off the interstate anywhere?

It is astonishing to learn that a building with an origin, life, and story as extraordinary as the Charles Sumner Greene House and Studio required rescue from demolition. Robinson Jeffers and Frank Lloyd Wright built their houses to last "a few hundred years." What of the others who were somewhat less deliberate? Is society willing to assume full responsibility for declaring and preserving historical, architectural, cultural, and, as in the case of Sea Urchin and Periwinkle, sites whose layers are archaeological treasures?

Carmel and many other cities and towns are acutely vulnerable to the pressures of demolition and development in this period of unprecedented prosperity. To preserve the village character of Carmel and elsewhere from the enthusiastic bulldozers of the new wealth, we must remind ourselves that we cherish certain places because we love those who founded them. Shall we all make Carmel part of our personal past? Its story is a chain mantra. As told by the poets it is the saga of passion; as told by the novelists it is a story of adventure; as told by journalists it is the story of painters of light and color and distant hills.

One can respond to Carmel without knowing its origins, but one cannot understand it. The intricacies of these origins can never be recreated and the legacy is a rich source of fascination. "Carmel" could not have occurred anywhere else on earth. Carmel, like all human habitations, has changed, is changing, will change. But how much can it change before it ceases to be Carmel?

Notes and Credits

≈ Notes

1 Sprio Kristov, *A History of Architcture*, "Settings and Rituals" (Oxford University Press: New York and Oxford, 1985), p. 447.

2 Lena Lencek and Gideon Bosker, *The Beach*, "The History of Paradise on Earth," (Viking: New York, 1998), p. 55.

3 Arnold Genthe, *As I Remember* (Reynal & Hitchcock: New York, 1936), p. 73.

4 Yi-Fu Tuan, *Topophilia*, "A Study on Environmental Perception, Attitudes, and Values," (Columbia University Press: New York, 1974), p. 248.

5 Lucy R. Lippard, *Overlay*, "Contemporary Art and the Art of Pre-History" (The New Press: New York, 1983), p. 160.

6 Robert Wernick, *LIFE* magazine, Vol. 62, No. 18, May 5, 1967, "Ideas in Houses," p. 105.